The Spirit Himself

by

Ralph M. Riggs

GOSPEL PUBLISHING HOUSE
Springfield, Missouri 65802

02-0590

THE SPIRIT HIMSELF beareth witness with our spirit, that we are children of God.

And in like manner the Spirit also helpeth our infirmity: for we know not how to pray as we ought; but THE SPIRIT HIMSELF maketh intercession for us with groanings which cannot be uttered.

Romans 8:16, 26
American Standard Version

First printing, 1950
Second printing, 1955
Third printing, 1957
Fourth printing, 1959
Fifth printing, 1960
Sixth printing, 1963
Seventh printing, 1965
Eighth printing, 1966
Ninth printing, 1968

[PRINTED
IN U.S.A.]

PREFACE

The ministers of the Pentecostal Movement have been so busy preaching the truths vouchsafed to them in these last days, that not many writers have taken time to set down in systematic form "these things which are most surely believed among us." There are now thousands of students in our Bible Institutes and Bible Colleges who must be taught, among the doctrines of Christianity, the distinctive doctrines of our Church. Our ministers likewise are in need of additional material relating to our distinctive testimony. Our laymen, too, may profit by having a new book concerning Pentecostal doctrine. To all these we ascribe and dedicate the following pages.

The notes from which this book has been written were prepared as studies in "Pentecostal Truth" for use in the 1948 Michigan Ministers' Seminar. To the ministers who constituted the class at this seminar goes credit for profitable discussion of the many matters which are dealt with herein.

We acknowledge assistance and guidance received from the authors mentioned in the Bibliography, many of whom we have quoted in these pages. Above all, to the Spirit Himself go our deepest gratitude and sincerest praise for the revelation of the truths which we believe He has granted us in this treatise.

TABLE OF CONTENTS

CONTENTS

CONTENTS

[ix]

CONTENTS

Introduction

PAUL'S DEFENSE AND OURS

"Men and brethren, I am a Pharisee, the son of a Pharisee." "But this I confess unto thee, that after the way which they call heresy, so worship I the God of my fathers." Acts 23:6; 24:14. Thus Paul defended himself before the Roman court to which he had been haled by his co-religionists. Before the bar of public opinion, the Pentecostal people have been arraigned by their fellow religionists of modern days. Like Paul they answer, "After the most straitest sect of our religion we have lived." Acts 26:5. Are they Christians? So are we. Are they Protestants? So are we. Are they Fundamentalists? So are we. Are they sincere, devout, and intense in the worship of the Lord Jesus Christ, as the only Savior and Hope of the world? We (we speak foolishly) are more so. cf. 2 Cor. 11:22, 23.

PENTECOSTAL PEOPLE ARE ORTHODOX

Among Pentecostal people there is not the slightest wavering concerning the divine authorship of the Scriptures. There is not one doubter among them concerning the creation of the world and all life by the fiat of God, as over against the popular heresy of evolution. The eternal deity of Christ, the only begotten Son of God; His virgin birth; His miracles; His vicarious death on Calvary; His physical resurrection from the dead, are all firmly believed by all Pentecostal people. The one defection that has come to our ranks has grown out of an over-emphasis of the doctrine of the deity of Christ. There is a group which is Pentecostal which now holds that there is only one person in the Godhead and His name is Jesus. This departure from orthodoxy is deplored by the great majority of Pentecostal people and fellowship has been withdrawn from this erring group. With this one exception, the Pentecostal ranks have been kept pure and unsullied by variation from standard orthodoxy; and the Pentecostal people can be said to be most intense and wholehearted in their worship, in their separation from the world, and in their evangelistic and missionary zeal.

THEY ARE COUNTED HERETICAL

Yet, it is "the way which they (others) call heresy." It is the sect that is everywhere spoken against. Acts 28:22. "Mine heritage is unto me as a speckled bird, the birds round about are against her." Jer 12:9. Estrangement, ostracism, and outright antagonism and attack have been its experience in the midst of its fellow Evangelicals. This is not out of line with that which the Bible describes as being the lot of the righteous. "Yea, and all that will live godly in Christ Jesus shall suffer persecution." 2 Tim. 3:12. "Woe unto you when all men shall speak well of you." Luke 6:26. Our only concern is lest it be our own faults for which we suffer, rather than purely for our religious faith and practice.

THE EXPLANATION

The reason for this estrangement and opposition lies largely in the fear of what is called *emotionalism* and in the lack of information concerning the doctrines of Pentecostals. Caricatures and excesses have also occurred, unfortunately, and these have caused a reaction which has naturally been unfavorable. All of this serves as a cloud to hide the work of God from those who should appreciate it, and constitutes a stumbling stone and rock of offense to shut out those who are not hungry enough for God to be willing to go without the camp bearing His reproach.

OUR APPEAL

There are many thousands who are sincere followers of our Lord and who believe in the ministry of the Holy Spirit, but who are strangers to the Pentecostal experience. It is to be regretted that the joy and power of the Baptism in the Holy Spirit and subsequent blessings have not yet been entered into by these friends. To them we extend a sincere hand of encouragement and assistance. We commend to their consideration the study of the Holy Spirit which follows. We ask only that they search the Scriptures to see if these things be so.

CHAPTER I

The Person of the Holy Spirit

SCRIPTURAL PROOF OF THE TRINITY

NO one can be a consistent believer of the Bible without holding the doctrine of the tri-unity of the Godhead. In addition to the numberless references to the different persons of the Godhead which are found throughout the whole Word of God, there are certain particular passages which refer to all three members of the Trinity. When Jesus was baptized in Jordan, John saw the *Holy Spirit* descending and heard a *voice from heaven* saying, "This is My *beloved Son* in whom *I* am well pleased." Matt. 3:16, 17. All three members of the Trinity are seen in the simultaneous yet distinct existence and operation. Jesus said, in John 14:16, "*I* will pray *the Father* and He shall give you another *Comforter.*" The three persons here mentioned cannot be denied as existing concurrently, and yet as different persons. The baptismal formula in Matt.

[1]

28:19, the apostolic benediction found in 2 Cor. 13:14, and the references in Acts 2:32, 33 and Acts 10:38 are further scriptures representing all three members of the Holy Trinity.

REASONABLE PROOF OF THE TRINITY

An additional proof of the existence of three persons in the Godhead is found in the fact that God is so complete, contains in His character such a wide range and broad compass of all virtues, and is such a perfect example in every respect, that it is necessary that there be a plurality of persons in the Godhead in order to contain and express it all. Strength, courage, humility, love, faith, hope, joy, peace, longsuffering, gentleness, goodness, meekness, righteousness, holiness, power, wisdom, truth, comfort, faithfulness, authority, companionship, service —all find perfect embodiment and expression in God. If the Godhead were only the sovereign Ruler, He could not have vacated His throne to become a helpless baby and to demonstrate the perfect humility which is inherent in His nature and which He manifested when He girded Himself and washed the disciples' feet. If there were no God the Son, then God the Father would have had no opportunity to have loved from the foundation of the world. In reality He could not even be the God of Love that He is, for there can be no love of others if there is no expression of it, and there could have been no expression of God's love had there not been other members of the Trinity upon whom to bestow it. Loving one's creatures who are His handiwork is a different kind of love than that which God expresses in His love for His "fellow," the Smitten Shepherd (Zech. 13:7); and there was a period of eternity in which there were no creatures. John 1:1, 2; Col. 1:15-17. How could He ever have descended to the "blackout" of Calvary, if there had been no God the Father in whom the Son could trust and who raised Him from the dead? These considerations are themselves proofs of the fact that there are distinct persons in the great infinite Godhead.

PERSONALITY OF THE HOLY SPIRIT

This membership of the Holy Spirit in the Holy Trinity is itself proof of the Personality of the Holy Spirit. Additional proof of His personality is found in the fact that the attributes of personality are manifested by Him. "He that searcheth the hearts knoweth what is *the mind* of the Spirit." Rom. 8:27. "But all these worketh that one and the selfsame Spirit, dividing to every man as *He will.*" 1 Cor. 12:11. "*Grieve* not the Holy Spirit of God." Eph. 4:30. "But they rebelled and *vexed* His Holy Spirit." Isa. 63:10. Thus we see that He has mind, will, and emotions.

Personal activities are also ascribed to Him. He strives with sinners. Gen. 6:3. He teaches. John 14:26. He testifies of Christ. John 15:26. He reproves. John 16:8. He guides. John 16:13; Rom. 8:14. He comforts. Acts 9:31. He helps our infirmities. Rom. 8:26. He intercedes for the saints. Rom. 8:26. He searches the deep things of God. 1 Cor. 2:10. He sanctifies. Rom. 15:16. He witnesses. Rom. 8:16. And He commands. Acts 16:6, 7. He is susceptible to personal treatment. He can be lied to. Acts 5:3. He can be resisted. Acts 7:51. He can be blasphemed. Matt. 12:31, 32. He can be grieved. Eph. 4:30. And He can be quenched. 1 Thess. 5:19.

DIFFERENCE BETWEEN PERSONALITY AND CORPOREITY

There are those who have difficulty in distinguishing between personality (being a person) and corporeity (having a body). They cannot understand or believe that anything which is invisible and intangible, and does not have a body, can be a person. Jesus said, "A spirit hath not flesh and bones, as ye see Me have." Luke 24:39. He also said, "God is a Spirit." John 4:24. It is recorded, "No man hath seen God at any time." John 1:18. Thus God exists as an invisible Spirit without flesh and bones. But the Creator and Ruler of a universe of persons must be Himself a person. The Holy Spirit is a spirit, like God the Father, and so the Holy Spirit is also a person. His omnipresence is an impossible conception if we confine Him to a body. Having the faculties and attributes of a person constitutes a person, whether or not that person customarily resides in a body.

NEED FOR GENUINE FAITH IN HIS PERSONALITY

Although accepted perfunctorily by orthodox Christians everywhere as theologically correct and true, the fact of the personality of the Holy Spirit needs emphasis and practical acceptance in the minds and hearts of believers. "I believe in the Holy Ghost" is easily repeated in church ceremony as creedal faith, but the truth is not so easy to comprehend or practice in one's personal life. The Holy Spirit IS a person. He is real. "I will pray the Father, and He shall give you ANOTHER Comforter, that He may abide with you forever." John 14:16. As Jesus had been real among them so that they heard Him with their ears, saw Him with their eyes, and handled Him with their hands, so now the Comforter was to take His place among them and, though invisible, be just as real a personal companion, friend, teacher, and guide.

MISTAKE TO USE "IT" WITH REFERENCE TO THE HOLY SPIRIT

The Holy Spirit must never be considered merely as a blessing, a feeling, or an influence. How far short of the full truth it is to refer to Him as "It." There are two verses in the King James Version of the Bible which use "It" in reference to the blessed Holy Spirit: Rom. 8:16, 26. This is doubtless a result of the use of the word "wind" or "breath" (which is in the neuter gender) as the name for the Spirit of God. Readers and translators had not become adjusted to the divine conception of the Breath of God constituting a distinct person, but now there should be no excuse for referring to the Holy Spirit as "It."

DEITY OF THE HOLY SPIRIT

That the Holy Spirit is very God is proven not only by His identification with God in the baptismal formula and apostolic benediction, but also in His possession of Godlike attributes. He is the eternal Spirit. Heb. 9:14. He is omnipresent. Psalm 139:7-10. He is omnipotent. Luke 1:37. And He is omniscient. 1 Cor. 2:10. Divine works are ascribed to Him. He shared in the creation of the world. Gen. 1:2. He creates new creatures in Christ. John 3:5; 2 Cor. 5:17. He raised Christ from the dead. Rom. 1:4; 8:11. His proceeding from the Father and from Christ (John 15:26; 16:7) also proves His deity.

CHAPTER II

The Names of the Holy Spirit

HE IS HUMBLE AND SELF-EFFACING

THE Holy Spirit is the member of the Trinity who is particularly self-effacing. He wrote, "This is life eternal that they might know Thee, the only true God, and Jesus Christ, whom Thou hast sent." John 17:3. He, too, gave us the picture of the eternal state, the city in which there is the throne of God and of the Lamb. Rev. 22:1. The fact that the Holy Spirit is not mentioned in connection with the other two members of the Trinity in these two passages does not imply His non-existence, but rather indicates His humility. Jesus told us that when the Holy Spirit came He would not speak of or by Himself. "He shall glorify me: for he shall receive of mine, and shall shew it unto you." John 16:14. He is thus content to serve in this hidden and, what some might call, subordinate capacity. Yet the importance of the person and work of the Holy Spirit is indicated by this declaration of Christ: "All manner of sin and blasphemy shall be forgiven unto men; but the blasphemy against the Holy Ghost shall not be forgiven unto men." Matt. 12:31.

"HOLY SPIRIT" PREFERRED TO "HOLY GHOST"

Some three hundred years ago, when the King James Version was first translated, the term "Holy Ghost" was most reverent and appropriate. Since then the use of the word "ghost" has narrowed down to a sense which makes its use in connection with the Holy Trinity out of place. The original word from which this translation has been made conveys simply the idea of wind or breath. To the minds of people today the word "spirit" is the proper word to express invisible personality. It is therefore the judgment of the translators of modern versions to replace the term "Holy Ghost" with the more fitting term "Holy Spirit."

FOUR MAJOR NAMES

There are four major names accorded to this third member of the Trinity. These are the Holy Spirit, the Spirit of God, the Spirit of Christ, and the Comforter. It must not be assumed or inferred that there is essential difference here, or that different persons are referred to by the use of these different names. These different terms merely call attention to certain functions or attributes which this same Person manifests on different occasions. As Christ

Himself is called Jesus, Redeemer, Savior, Son of God, Son of Man, Prince of Peace, Word of God, Bridegroom, King of kings, Lord of lords, Apostle, High Priest, Shepherd, etc., to indicate various functions and relations which He possesses, so it is consistent and proper that different names be used in connection with the Holy Spirit.

1. THE HOLY SPIRIT.

The Holy Spirit is referred to as "The Spirit" in a number of Scriptural passages. "And hereby we know that He abideth in us, by the Spirit which He hath given us." 1 John 3:24. "The Spirit searcheth all things, yea, the deep things of God." 1 Cor. 2:10. But the name which is most frequently accorded the third person of the Trinity is "the Holy Spirit." It is true that this blessed Person has many other characteristics, very prominent among which is His humility or self-effacement. But He is never called the Humble Spirit. Predominantly He is referred to as "the Holy Spirit."

Emphasis on Holiness.

He shares with other members of the Trinity all the attributes and qualities of God. When Isaiah saw the Lord high and lifted up, the seraphim cried one to another, saying, "Holy, Holy, Holy is the Lord of Hosts," one "holy" apparently for each member of the Trinity. Isa. 6:3. When John saw the throne set in heaven and Him who sat upon it, the four living creatures cried, saying, "Holy, Holy,

Holy, Lord God Almighty, which was, and is, and is to come." Rev. 4:8. God told Moses, as quoted by Peter, "Be ye holy, for I am holy." Lev. 11:44; 1 Peter 1:16. But nevertheless it is the third person of the Holy Trinity who is particularly designated as "holy." This indicates that in Him rests the blazing fire of the purity and holiness of Almighty God. The first thing that must be expected in dealing with the Holy Spirit is that He will uncover and condemn sin in the life. John 16:8. This is His major ministry. By Him also the believer is enabled to live a life of victory over sin. Holiness therefore is the outstanding characteristic of this member of the Trinity.

2. SPIRIT OF GOD.

Quite often in the Word of God the Holy Spirit is referred to as the Spirit of God. "Grieve not the Holy Spirit of God, by which ye are sealed unto the day of redemption." Eph. 4:30. "Hereby know ye the Spirit of God." 1 John 4:2. By the use of this name in referring to the Holy Spirit, particular attention is called to the fact that He has a specific relation to God the Father. Jesus told us that the Holy Spirit proceeds from the Father. "And when the Comforter is come, whom I will send unto you from the Father, even the Spirit of Truth, which proceedeth from the Father, He shall testify of Me." John 15:26. The fact then that He proceeds from the Father justifies this name, "the Spirit of God."

THE NAMES

a. Draws Men to Christ.

In the capacity of the Spirit of God, the Holy Spirit does the work of the Father here on earth. Jesus said, "No man can come to Me, except the Father which hath sent Me draw him." John 6:44. When the Holy Spirit came, He took up this particular activity of the Father, and now it is He who reproves the world of sin and of righteousness and of judgment. It is "through the sanctification of the Spirit" that men are chosen to salvation. 2 Thess. 2:13. Through this same "sanctification of the Spirit" they are brought unto obedience and sprinkling of the blood of Jesus Christ. 1 Peter 1:2.

b. Reveals Truth.

When Peter made his immortal confession, "Thou art the Christ, the Son of the Living God," Jesus said, "Blessed art thou, Simon Bar-jona, for flesh and blood hath not revealed it unto thee, but my Father which is in heaven." Matt. 16:17. On another occasion, Jesus said, "I thank Thee, O Father, Lord of heaven and earth, because Thou hast hid these things from the wise and prudent, and hast revealed them unto babes." Matt. 11:25. Thus, preceding the day of Pentecost, it was the Father's work to reveal truth to men. "Howbeit, when He the Spirit of Truth, is come, He will guide you into all truth." John 16:13. "He shall teach you all things, and bring all things to your remembrance whatsoever I have said unto you." John 14:26.

Here again we see that the Spirit of God does the work of God on the earth today.

c. Guides.

When Jesus was on earth it was the Father who gave Him commandment what He should do and what He should speak. John 12:49-50. He walked in the light of His Father, and He did only those things which He saw His Father do. John 11:9; 5:19. Now that the Holy Spirit is come, it is He who does this work of the Father in the life of believers. "As many as are led by the Spirit of God, they are the sons of God." Rom. 8:14.

d. Disciplines.

Jesus called attention to the fact that while He is the vine and we are the branches, the Father is the Husbandman. "Every branch in Me that beareth not fruit HE taketh away; and every branch that beareth fruit, HE purgeth it, that it may bring forth more fruit." John 15:2. "Whom the Lord loveth He chasteneth, and scourgeth every son whom He receiveth." Heb. 12:6. It is the work of the Father to discipline believers. Isaiah tells us that the Lord shall wash away the filth of the daughters of Zion and shall purge the blood of Jerusalem from the midst thereof by "the spirit of judgment and by the spirit of burning." Isa. 4:4. Thus the disciplinary work of the Father is carried on in the lives of believers by the blessed Holy Spirit.

3. SPIRIT OF CHRIST.

The Holy Spirit is also referred to as the Spirit of Christ. "Now if any man have not the Spirit of Christ, he is none of His." Rom. 8:9. When this term is used, attention is called to the fact that He was given by Christ. "If I go not away, the Comforter will not come unto you; but if I depart, *I* will send Him unto you." John 16:7. Jesus appeared unto them the night of the resurrection, breathed on them and said, "Receive ye the Holy Ghost." John 20:22. In his sermon on the day of Pentecost, Peter declared, "This Jesus hath God raised up, whereof we all are witnesses. Therefore being by the right hand of God exalted, and having received of the Father the promise of the Holy Ghost, HE hath shed forth this, which ye now see and hear." Acts 2:32, 33. Thus we see that the Holy Spirit is sent into the world by Christ.

a. *Imparts Christ-life.*

In the capacity of being sent by Christ, He comes to impart the Christ-life. "For the law of the Spirit of life in Christ Jesus hath made me free from the law of sin and death." Rom. 8:2. In 1 John 5:11, 12 we are told that "this life is in His Son. He that hath the Son hath life; and he that hath not the Son of God hath not life." Life is in the Son of God and the Spirit of Christ is called the Spirit of Life. Jesus told Nicodemus, "Except a man be born of water and of the Spirit, he cannot enter into the kingdom of God." John 3:5. The impartation of the Christ-life is the work of the Spirit of Christ.

b. Produces Christ-fruits.

Paul tells us in Phil. 1:11 that the fruits of righteousness are by Jesus Christ. The *Christ-life* within is the seedbed from which there arise and are produced various kinds of Christian fruit. The same writer tells us in Gal. 5:22-23 that "the fruit of the *Spirit* is love, joy, peace, longsuffering, gentleness, goodness, faith, meekness, temperance." Thus it is the work of the Holy Spirit as the Spirit of Christ to develop the Christ-life within the believer in the production of the various qualities which are called the fruit of the Spirit.

c. Reveals Things of Christ.

Another beautiful ministry of the Holy Spirit as the Spirit of Christ is the taking of the things of Christ and showing them to us. "He shall glorify me; for he shall receive of mine and shall shew it unto you." John 16:14. Our Lord came to set us a perfect example of Christian living. He walked in the pathway in which we are commanded to follow. He put Himself on our level and was in all points tempted like as we are yet without sin. He demonstrated how to walk acceptably with God. He made distinct revelation of this art and frankly declared what was involved in its accomplishment. We will find this especially in the 4th to the 17th chapters of John. To those who will listen, the blessed Holy Spirit will glorify Christ by taking these "things of Christ" and revealing their wonder and beauty to them. As we hereby learn the mystery of Christ and the secret of the success of His wonderful life, we are enabled to walk in that same pathway and partake of that same glorious victory.

d. Imparts Power of Christ.

Possibly the most triumphant of all of the ministries of the Holy Spirit as He comes to us from Christ is to bring a mighty baptism of power. Jesus said, "All *power* is given unto Me in Heaven and in earth." Matt. 28:18. Paul declared Christ to be the very *power* of God. 1 Cor. 1:24. The outstanding characteristic of the baptism in the Holy Spirit as promised by Christ is that it would be an enduement with *power* from on high. Luke 24:49. "But ye shall receive *power,* after that the Holy Ghost is come upon you." Acts 1:8. "He that believeth on Me, the works that I do shall he do also; and greater works than these shall he do; because I go unto my Father" [and will send you back the Spirit of power]. John 14:12.

e. Takes Place of Christ.

"And I will pray the Father and He shall give you ANOTHER Comforter, that he may abide with you forever." John 14:16. This is the promise of Christ that the Holy Spirit would take His place in their lives. He was to fill the place which Jesus had occupied and was about to vacate. The Holy Spirit was to be to them a personal friend, a wonderful teacher, a very real companion, and guide. He was to be a Person in every sense of the word and just such a Person as Jesus had been. It is in this capacity that the Holy Spirit wishes to serve and is meant to serve in the lives of all believers. He should be dominant, real, personal, and completely satisfying.

4. COMFORTER.

The name which Christ Himself used in announcing the coming of the Holy Spirit is "the Comforter." John 14:16. In no other place in the Scripture is the Holy Spirit referred to by this gracious title. The hearts of the disciples were troubled. They were in need of divine comfort. Jesus supplied this need by the promise of the gift of Him who would bring abundant comfort to their hearts. The comfort which He would bring would not merely be sympathy but would effect a complete healing of their wounded hearts by the impartation of courage and strength. This ministry He should have in the lives of all believers. Acts 9:31.

a. Paraclete.

The word "paracletos," which is here translated "Comforter," means more than one who comforts. He is one who walks alongside or is a companion. As Paraclete, the Holy Spirit is one who is ready to provide strength, courage, wisdom, and grace in any form. He supplies all that a loving, capable companion would be asked to supply to satisfy every longing and need of the human heart.

b. Communion of the Holy Spirit.

"The grace of our Lord Jesus Christ, and the love of God, and the communion of the Holy Ghost be with you all." 2 Cor. 13:14. This grace of our Lord and the love of God are brought to us by the Holy Spirit. Communing with the Holy Spirit, having fellowship with Him, letting Him perform His appointed ministry in our lives, brings to us the fullness of the blessing of God. The benediction of the Holy Trinity thus rests upon us.

CHAPTER III

The Seven Spirits of God

THERE IS ONE SPIRIT

"THERE is one body, and one Spirit, even as ye are called in one hope of your calling." Eph. 4:4. This is a declaration of the unity of the Holy Spirit. He is a distinct person with a unique personality of His own. It is true that He is called the Spirit of God and the Spirit of Christ as well as the Holy Spirit. These are His outstanding titles. But He is one person performing different ministries.

THERE ARE SEVEN SPIRITS

Believing in the unity of the Holy Spirit, we can now look at Rev. 1:4; 4:5; and 5:6. "John to the seven churches which are in Asia: Grace be unto you, and peace, from him which is, and which was, and which is to come, and from the *seven* Spirits which are before his throne." "And out of the throne proceeded lightnings and thunderings and voices: and there were seven lamps of fire burning before

the throne, which are the seven Spirits of God."
"And I beheld, and lo, in the midst of the throne
and of the four beasts, and in the midst ~of the
elders, stood a Lamb as it had been slain, having
seven horns and seven eyes, which are the seven
Spirits of God sent forth into all the earth." Here we
have reference to the *seven* Spirits of God. We must
not consider these a contradiction of Eph. 4:4. The
unity of the Spirit finds expression in seven distinctive ways. The supreme God is One in very
truth (Deut. 6:4), and yet the Bible sets forth
that there are three distinct persons in the Godhead.
In like manner the Holy Spirit is a unity, but there
are seven expressions or forms in which He operates
among men. As the candlestick of the wilderness
tabernacle was made of one piece of beaten gold
and had seven branches and lamps (Ex. 25:31-37),
so the Holy Spirit is one and yet shines forth upon
the world in seven different ways.

THE SPIRIT OF GRACE.

In Heb. 10:29 reference is made to the Spirit of
grace. The whole Gospel is a gospel of grace. God
so loved that He gave freely. The Lord Jesus Christ
offers His gifts purely as a matter of grace. "For
by grace are ye saved through faith; and that not
of yourselves: it is the gift of God; not of works,
lest any man should boast." Eph. 2:8, 9. In perfect
conformity, therefore, to the Father and the Son, and
bringing to the world their one Spirit and pro-
posal of grace, the Holy Spirit presents Heaven's

[19]

treasures as gracious gifts to men. He refuses to deal with those who would barter with Him. He will accept no remuneration for His services. He will allow not one scintilla of merit or credit to be presented to Him in payment for His gifts. Grace is the fundamental law of His ministry. There is no limit to what He will give and do as we accept it as unmerited favor. He is especially the Spirit of grace.

THE SPIRIT OF LIFE.

Particularly as the Spirit of Christ He operates in the lives of believers as the Spirit of life. Rom. 8:2. "And the Spirit of God moved upon the face of the waters" (Gen. 1:2), infusing life in the old or first creation. He is now busy imparting life to bring into existence the new creation. 2 Cor. 5:17. "Now if any man have not the Spirit of Christ, he is none of His." Rom. 8:9. Being the Spirit of Christ, He the Spirit of life, makes us free from the law of sin and death. Rom. 8:2. He is the stream of divine life which flows into our members overwhelming the law of sin and death, coursing through us with virtue from on high. This is more abundant life, and it comes to us in the person of the Holy Spirit.

The Spirit of Life in Our Bodies.

This life is not only for our souls and spiritual natures. As we will receive it, the Spirit of life can and will penetrate our physical bodies and quicken them. Rom. 8:11. There is divine healing as the gift of the Holy Spirit. 1 Cor. 12:9. There is divine health by the same Holy Spirit. 2 Cor. 4: 10, 11. There is even superhuman strength, as it is needed, by this same Holy Spirit. It was the Spirit of the Lord that came mightily upon Samson which enabled him to perform superhuman feats. Judges 14:6, 19. The same Spirit caught away Philip and transported him to a distant point. Acts 8:39, 40. This operation of the Holy Spirit should not be overlooked or neglected. He will not have been allowed to perform His full ministry in our lives unless we drink of the well of divine life, both for soul and body.

THE SPIRIT OF ADOPTION.

It is not in vain that the Holy Spirit is called the Spirit of *adoption*. Rom. 8:15. The special work of establishing former sons of Satan in the family of God as His legal heirs is a particular ministry of the Holy Spirit.[1] He has been assigned the task

---

[1]In this connection, Frank M. Boyd, well-known Pentecostal author and teacher, comments:

"The word 'adoption' in the Greek original is an interesting word, meaning literally 'the placing of sons.' It comes from two words 'huios'—Son, and 'thesis'—a placing.

"Our birth into the family of God is rather expressed by another Greek word 'teknon,' a word which John uses frequently to express a relation based upon community of nature. He never uses the word 'huios' to describe the relation of Christians to God, since he regards their position not as a result of *adoption*, but of a *new life*.

"Paul, on the contrary, regards the relation from the legal

of effecting our adoption and persuading us who have been brought from the family of sin into the family of God that we are actually and legally adopted into His family. It is with some temerity that we approach our Father's throne, even though we have been urged to come boldly to the Throne of Grace. Heb. 4:16. Our unbelief takes the guise of false humility, and we secretly compliment ourselves upon our hesitation to take hold of the promises of God. But we must clearly understand that God will not approve of our unbelief. He is far rather pleased by our bold assertion of our place as full-fledged children of His family. It is the distinct work of the Holy Spirit to encourage and coach us along these lines.

---

standpoint, as *adoption,* imparting a new dignity and relation. Rom. 8:15; Gal. 4:5, 6.

"The whole thought of *adoption* is that we now stand in a completeness of relation to God as sons, which makes us 'heirs of God and joint-heirs with Jesus Christ'—He, the only-begotten Son, and we, the 'many sons' whom He is bringing to glory. Heb. 2:10.

"It is the ministry of the blessed Holy Spirit to actualize that sonship (Gal. 4:7) and to inspire us with the utmost confidence in our approach to God.

"One day, as Paul indicates in Rom. 8:23, we shall enter into the consummation of 'adoption' by the redemption of our bodies (Rom. 8:23), when we shall be *manifested as sons* (Rom. 8:19) before the wondering heavenly hosts; and all creation will rejoice in what God has wrought through grace in redeeming a fallen race."

THE SPIRIT OF HOLINESS.

In addition to the Holy Spirit's having as His distinctive name the *Holy* Spirit, it is definitely recorded that He is the Spirit of Holiness. Rom. 1:4. Isaiah declares He is the spirit of *judgment* and the Spirit of *burning*. Isa. 4:4. The filth of the daughters of Zion and the blood which was upon that holy city were washed away and purged from the midst thereof by the spirit of judgment and by the spirit of burning. God is the enemy of sin wherever He finds it. In the heart of the believer He attacks it immediately. The Spirit of Holiness, as the spirit of judgment, uncovers and condemns all that is wrong, and, as the spirit of burning, purges it out. This is a work which is not so pleasant to the believer, but is very vital to the program of God. The Bride of the Lamb must be a glorious church, without spot or wrinkle or any such thing. She must be holy and without blemish. Hence the Holy Spirit is busy sanctifying and cleansing her with the washing of water by the Word. To be filled with the Holy Spirit means to allow the Holy Spirit to search out, and condemn, and destroy all the impurities of the nature and spirit.

Holiness Is a Spirit.

The phrase, "Spirit of Holiness," reveals to us that holiness is not merely a state of grace or a sanctifying act. There is a divine person who is the Spirit of Holiness from whom there emanates the quality of holiness which is to be shed abroad with-

[23]

in our lives. As the tree is sustained by the life within and will lose its freshness and, shortly, its very life unless life flows in its trunk out to its leaves, just so holiness will be an empty, rattling exterior and mere profession, unless it is energized and vitalized constantly by Him who is the Spirit of Holiness. Christ, too, is made unto us sanctification, for, in the words of Gabriel, He also is "that holy thing." Luke 1:35. A Person within one's life then is the secret of true holiness and the Holy Spirit of Holiness is that Person.

THE SPIRIT OF SUPPLICATIONS.

In Zechariah 12:10, the Holy Spirit is referred to as the spirit of supplications. Paul tells us, "Likewise the Spirit also helpeth our infirmities: for we know not what we should pray for as we ought: but the Spirit Himself maketh intercession for us with groanings which cannot be uttered. And he that searcheth the hearts knoweth what is the mind of the Spirit, because he maketh intercession for the saints according to the will of God." Rom. 8:26-27. More specifically in 1 Cor. 14:2 we are instructed that "he that speaketh in an unknown tongue speaketh not unto men, but unto God: for no man understandeth him; howbeit in the spirit he speaketh mysteries." Paul says, "For if I pray in an unknown tongue, my spirit prayeth, but my understanding is unfruitful. What is it then? I will pray with the spirit, and I will pray with the understanding also: I will sing with the spirit, and I will sing with the understanding also." vv. 14, 15. This particularly designates the gift of tongues as a ministry of prayer in the spirit. The Holy Spirit is so efficient and capable, by reason of the fact that He is God Himself and knoweth all things, that He is pre-eminently qualified to control and guide the prayer life of the believer. Speaking through the Spirit-filled saints in the gift of the unknown tongue or by inspiring the human understanding, He is the mighty spirit of supplications. How great is the need for believers to be filled with the spirit of supplications. How much more could be accomplished for God these days if Spirit-filled people would yield themselves to the mighty ministry of intercession as the spirit of supplications Himself prayed through them according to the will of God.

THE SPIRIT OF TRUTH.

We come now to the revelation of the Holy Spirit as the spirit of truth. John 16:13. In Isaiah's prophecy of the coming of Messiah as recorded in ch. 11:2-3a, the Spirit of the Lord is referred to as "the spirit of *wisdom* and *understanding*, the spirit of *counsel* and *might*, the spirit of *knowledge* and of the *fear of the Lord*: And shall make him of *quick understanding in the fear of the Lord.*" Here is a sevenfold expression of the spirit of truth. This is the only one of these seven Spirits of God which itself has a sevenfold definition. This is to call our particular attention to the high importance of this phase of the Spirit's activity. When Christ was informing the disciples concerning the coming of the Comforter who was to take His place alongside of the disciples, His chief emphasis concerning the work and ministry of that comforter was that He would TEACH them all things. John 14:26; 16:13. It is Christ who gave Him the title of the spirit of truth. He also stated that when the spirit of truth was come He should testify of Him. John 15:26. Since Christ is Himself the truth (John 14:6), it is to be expected that the spirit of truth would testify of the Christ who is truth. For the third time Jesus calls the Holy Spirit the spirit of truth in John 16:13. Here He declares He will guide you into all truth. Again He says that He shall take of Mine and shall show it unto you.

Teaching, the Work of the Spirit.

In 1 Cor. 12:28; Rom. 12:7; and Eph. 4:11, it is set forth that teaching is a manifestation and a gift of the Holy Spirit. Thus we have this heavy emphasis in different parts of the Bible concerning the Spirit's ministry of teaching. This is predominantly the work of the Holy Spirit. "My people are destroyed for lack of knowledge." Hosea 4:6. Knowledge is light and permits proper adjustment to the facts of life. The spiritual realm is uncharted, and yet it is the sphere through which we must find our way in order to have power over sin, the world, and the devil, come out victorious in the struggle of life, and land safely on heaven's shore. How are we to find our way through this uncharted realm!

[26]

A *guide* has been sent us, none other than a member of the Divine Trinity Himself, who will take us by the hand and lead us carefully and faithfully into full and complete understanding of the perfect will of God and bring us into the place of personal victory and power. The Holy Spirit calls individuals into the ministry of teaching. He ministers also directly in the Spirit-taught life. How important it is and how we need to let the Holy Spirit have His way in our study of the Bible, our application to divine learning, and our entry into all truth.

THE SPIRIT OF GLORY.

Fittingly, the last of the seven Spirits of God is the spirit of glory. "If ye then be reproached for the name of Christ, happy are ye: for the spirit of glory and of God resteth upon you: on their part he is evil spoken of, but on your part he is glorified." 1 Peter 4:14. "For I reckon that the sufferings of this present time are not worthy to be compared with the glory which shall be revealed in us." Rom. 8:18. Surely there is a relationship and a corresponding ratio here. Suffer for Him and the spirit of glory rests upon you: suffer for Him and glory is wrought within you to be revealed at the last time. Through and by the wounds of body and spirit, the spirit of glory works His glory into our lives and stores it up for the day of redemption. By this means our own glorification is being provided for and by this means also our Lord is glorified ("on your part He is glorified"). This was the Spirit that rested upon Stephen as his enemies gnashed on him with their teeth and prepared to stone him. Acts 7:55. Stephen was glorified, for the Lord stood up to receive him. Christ was glorified by the valiant loyalty and devotion of His servant.

CHAPTER IV

The Holy Spirit in the Old Testament

THROUGHOUT THE OLD TESTAMENT

FROM the study of the nature of the Holy Spirit as revealed by His names, let us now trace the work and presence of the Holy Spirit in the Old Testament. It may come as a surprise to many to learn that the Holy Spirit is mentioned eighty-one times in the Old Testament. This is one third as many times as He is mentioned in the New Testament. Thirteen of these Old Testament references are found in the Pentateuch; and Isaiah and Ezekiel have fourteen and twelve passages respectively. Judges and First Samuel each has seven references, and the book of the Psalms has five. There are only sixteen books out of the thirty-nine books of the Old Testament which do not have a reference to the Holy Spirit.

AT CREATION

The Holy Spirit is called, in Heb. 9:14, "the eternal Spirit." This is a declaration of the fact that the Holy Spirit has existed from all eternity. The plural form of the Hebrew word for God (Elohim) found in Gen. 1:1 presents the thought that the Holy Spirit is included in the Deity who created the world in the beginning. As that Deity conferred among Themselves saying, "Let us make man," it is again implied that the Holy Spirit was present at the Creation. This creative activity is specifically declared in Gen. 1:2. "The Spirit of God moved upon the face of the waters."

WITH ANTEDILUVIANS

"My Spirit will not always strive with man." Gen. 6:3. Here is a revelation of a ministry of the Holy Spirit in the Old Testament which is similar to, if not the same as, that which He has in the New Testament. He now reproves the world of sin and draws men unto Christ. Before the flood He had striven with men and had secured the loyal following of Enoch and the godly line. But at the time of the flood only Noah and his family were righteous. All others were finally impenitent. One hundred and twenty years more of His striving and then judgment.

JOSEPH AND BEZALEEL

There are many instances of the special visitation of the Holy Spirit in the Old Testament days, upon individuals who were thus equipped to perform certain functions. The Spirit of the Lord indwelt Joseph, enabling him to understand the dreams of Pharaoh and to administer the affairs of state. Gen. 41:38; Acts 7:9, 10. In the erection of the holy tabernacle in the wilderness, the Holy Spirit came upon Bezaleel, who was "filled with the Spirit of God in wisdom and in understanding and in knowledge and in all manner of workmanship to devise cunning works, to work in gold and in silver and in brass, and in cutting of stones to set them, and in carving of timber, to work all manner of workmanship." Ex. 31:1-6; 35:30-35.

MOSES, JOSHUA, THE SEVENTY ELDERS, AND THE JUDGES

Moses was filled with the Holy Spirit. Isaiah tells us so. Isa. 63:11. And since it is written that the spirit which indwelt Moses was conveyed to the seventy elders, so that the Holy Spirit "rested upon them," it is clearly proven that Moses was a man who was filled with the Holy Spirit. Num. 11:17, 25. It is recorded of Joshua in Num. 27:18 and Deut. 34:9 that he was a man in whom was the Spirit. The Word tells us, too, that certain judges were visited by the Holy Spirit as enablement for the accomplishment of their tasks. The statement concerning Othniel is found in Judges 3:10; concerning Gideon in Judges 6:34; concerning Jephthah in Judges 11:29; and concerning Samson in Judges 13:25; 14:6, 19; and 15:14.

SAUL AND DAVID

When the time came that Israel desired a king, God gave them Saul, a son of Kish, and equipped him for his work by the Holy Spirit's coming upon him. 1 Sam. 10:6, 10; 11:6; 19:23. Notice also that the Spirit of the Lord departed from Saul after that willful king continually disobeyed. 1 Sam. 16:14. His successor, David, likewise received the Spirit of the Lord as the anointing for kingship. 1 Sam. 16:13. David feared lest he, too, lose the Holy Spirit as a result of his sin and prayed earnestly that the Lord would not take away His Holy Spirit from him. Psa. 51:11.

THE PROPHETS

In connection with Saul's receiving the Holy Spirit at the beginning and during his reign, it is recorded (1 Sam. 10:5, 6 and 19:20-24) that there was a company of prophets who did prophesy. All through the history of the children of Israel thereafter there arose the prophets (Isaiah to Malachi) who prophesied under the anointing of the Holy Spirit. 1 Peter 1:11 and Neh. 9:30 declare that these prophets were indwelt by the Spirit of Christ. We are told also that "these holy men of God spake as they were moved by the Holy Ghost." 2 Peter 1:21. Micah declared, "I am full of power by the Spirit of the Lord." Micah 3:8. And through Zechariah (4:6) came the eternal principle: "Not by might, nor by power, but by my Spirit, saith the Lord of hosts." There were also prophets and holy men other than those whose messages are recorded to whom the word of the Lord came: Nathan, 2 Sam. 12:1; Gad, 2 Sam. 24:11; Elijah, 1 Kings 17:1, 2; Elisha, 2 Kings 2:21; Amasai, 1 Chron. 12:18; Azariah, 2 Chron. 15:1; Jahaziel, 2 Chron. 20:14; Zechariah, 2 Chron. 24:20.

THE HOLY SPIRIT PROPHESIED

We call attention to the fact that the visitation of the Holy Spirit upon certain individuals in the Old Testament resulted in *prophesying* by those thus visited. This was true in the case of the seventy elders who received of the spirit of Moses as recorded in Numbers 11:16, 17, 25-29. The prophets of 1 Sam. 10:5-11 prophesied, as did Saul, when the Holy Spirit came upon them. This was the peculiar manifestation of the Holy Spirit as He came upon the prophets of old. They spake as they were moved by the Holy Ghost.

HE WAS WITH ALL ISRAEL

The general ministry of the Holy Spirit to and with the children of Israel is referred to in detail in Isa. 63:9-14. This is confirmed in Neh. 9:20 and Hag. 2:5. In the review given above we have seen that the Holy Spirit was present in the Old Testament enduing those who were called to serve in some distinctive capacity. Although He led the entire group, yet His particular anointing and blessing rested here and there upon outstanding individuals.

[33]

PREDICTION OF GENERAL OUTPOURING

While this was the experience of the Israelites in the Old Testament, there were various prophets who foretold the time when there would be a general, universal diffusion of the Holy Spirit. Joel puts it into definite words: "And it shall come to pass afterward that I will pour out my Spirit upon all flesh: and your sons and your daughters shall prophesy, your old men shall dream dreams, your young men shall see visions: and also upon the servants and upon the handmaids in those days will I pour out my spirit." Joel 2:28, 29. This foretells the outpouring of the Holy Spirit *upon all flesh,* extending to all people the experience which had come in Israelitish history to individuals here and there. This visitation was to be upon all flesh, Jew and Gentile, sons and daughters, and old men and young men. There would come such a mighty outpouring of the Holy Spirit that they all would prophesy. This then is the prediction that the special visitation of the Holy Spirit upon individuals in the Old Testament time, which caused them to prophesy would, at a later time, come upon all flesh, causing them also to PROPHESY. Peter announced on the day of Pentecost that the outpouring there on the one hundred and twenty disciples (who included the apostles; certain women; Mary, the mother of Jesus; and her other sons, who had now become disciples) was a direct fulfillment of Joel's prophecy. Acts 2:16. The prophecy concerning the general outpouring of the Holy Spirit upon all flesh, which Joel stated so clearly, is also made, though in less definite terms, by Isaiah (28:11, 12 32:15; 44:3) by Ezekiel (36:27), and by Jeremiah (31:31-34).

MESSIAH TO BE SPIRIT - FILLED

The Messiah who was to come was Himself particularly to minister under the anointing of the Holy Spirit. Isaiah declared, "And there shall come forth a rod out of the stem of Jesse, and a Branch shall grow out of his roots: and the Spirit of the Lord shall rest upon him, the spirit of wisdom and understanding, the spirit of counsel and might, the spirit of knowledge and of the fear of the Lord and shall make him of quick understanding in the fear of the Lord; and he shall not judge after the sight of his eyes, neither reprove after the hearing of his ears." Isa. 11:1-3. In the 61st chapter of Isaiah he represents the Messiah as saying: "The Spirit of the Lord God is upon me, because the Lord hath anointed me to preach good tidings unto the meek: He hath sent me to bind up the broken-hearted, to proclaim liberty to the captives, and the opening of the prison to them that are bound." v. 1.

SUMMARY

Thus we see that the Holy Spirit came upon certain individuals in the Old Testament time. It was predicted also that the time would come when He would similarly be poured out on all flesh; and it was further prophesied that He would rest mightily upon the coming Messiah.

CHAPTER V

The Holy Spirit in the Time of Christ

AT THE BIRTH OF JOHN THE BAPTIST AND OF JESUS

WE come now to the New Testament era and notice certain visitations of the Holy Spirit which preceded the day of Pentecost. Gabriel informed Zacharias that the son which was to be given to him in his old age would be filled with the Holy Spirit from his mother's womb. Luke 1:15. The same angel told Mary that the Holy Spirit would come upon her and thus that Holy Thing which should be born of her would be called the Son of God. Luke 1:35. When Mary went to visit her cousin Elisabeth, Elisabeth was filled with the Holy Spirit and spoke with a loud voice. vv. 41-42. Zacharias, at the birth of John, was filled with the Holy Spirit and prophesied. v.

67. Who would deny that Mary, the mother of Jesus, herself was filled with the Holy Spirit as she broke out in the beautiful Magnificat of Luke 1:46-55? There was also a man in Jerusalem whose name was Simeon, and "the Holy Ghost was upon him." It was revealed unto him by the Holy Spirit that he should not see death until he had seen the Lord Christ. He also "came by the Spirit into the temple." Luke 2:25-27. Anna too was a prophetess who "gave thanks likewise unto the Lord." Thus we have eight distinct references to the Holy Spirit in the first two chapters of Luke, with accompanying "crying out" and "prophesying" under the power of the Holy Spirit.

IN JESUS' MINISTRY

At the River Jordan, John the Baptist was given a sign by Him who sent him to baptize with water, saying, "Upon whom thou shalt see the Spirit descending and remaining on him, the same is he which baptizeth with the Holy Ghost." "And John bare record, saying, I saw the Spirit descending from heaven like a dove, and it abode upon him." John 1:32, 33. Peter referred to this experience in Acts 10:38. "How God anointed Jesus of Nazareth with the Holy Ghost and with power; who went about doing good and healing all that were oppressed of the devil; for God was with him." His very name "Christ" means "the anointed one." Thus the prediction of Isaiah concerning the Messiah being anointed with the Holy Spirit was fulfilled. Jesus confirmed this specifically in the synagogue at Nazareth, where He read Isaiah 61:1, 2 and declared, "This day is this scripture fulfilled in your ears." Luke 4:21. Jesus was baptized in the Holy Spirit (Matt. 3:16); was driven by the Holy Spirit into the wilderness (Mark 1:12); returned in the power of the Spirit into Galilee (Luke 4:14); by the Spirit of God cast out devils (Matt. 12:28); through the Eternal Spirit offered himself without spot to God (Heb. 9:14); and through the Holy Spirit gave commandment unto the apostles whom He had chosen. Acts 1:2.

PREDICTION BY JOHN THE BAPTIST OF GENERAL OUTPOURING

John the Baptist also prophesied that Jesus would be the instrument for the diffusion of the Holy Spirit that Joel had predicted. "I indeed baptize you with water; but one mightier than I cometh, the latchet of whose shoes I am not worthy to unloose: he shall baptize you with the Holy Ghost and with fire." Luke 3:16.

CHRIST'S PREDICTION OF THE SPIRIT'S COMING

As Christ approached the end of His ministry and prepared to lay down His leadership and to finish teaching His disciples, He introduced them to the truth of the coming of the Holy Spirit. He had referred to that coming in John 4:14 as the "well of water" and in John 7:37-38 as "rivers of water" flowing from the innermost parts of those who believed on Him. In Luke 11:13 He said that His Father would give the Holy Spirit to them that asked Him. In John 14:16 He declared: "And I will pray the Father and he shall give you another Comforter, that he may abide with you forever." Throughout His farewell discourse to His disciples, He referred many times to the coming of the Holy Spirit and defined something of the ministry which that coming Holy Spirit would perform. John 14:17, 26; 15:26; 16:7-15.

CHRIST BREATHED THE HOLY SPIRIT UPON THE DISCIPLES

This brings us up to the time of the crucifixion and resurrection of Christ and the approaching day of Pentecost. On the day of His resurrection, as soon as He had risen in His glory and had become the glorified Christ, He breathed upon His disciples and said, "Receive ye the Holy Ghost." John 20:22. This could not have been the fulfillment of Old Testament prophecies and those of John the Baptist and of Jesus Himself concerning the outpouring of the Holy Spirit. For forty days later, in Acts 1:4-5, He commanded His disciples to wait for the promise of the Father, declaring that they would yet be baptized with the Holy Ghost not many days hence. He described the effect of that baptism in Acts 1:8, and in the 9th verse it is stated that when He had spoken these things He was taken up, and a cloud received Him out of their sight. Thus, forty days after the night of the resurrection when He had breathed upon them, saying, "Receive ye the Holy Ghost," He represented the baptism of the Holy Spirit as still future. The reception of the Holy Spirit, then, by the disciples on the night of the resurrection, was a distinct experience, but must not be confused or made identical with the baptism of the Holy Spirit which came upon them on the day of Pentecost. A study in the following chapter of "the Holy Spirit in conversion" will explain to us the meaning of Christ's breathing on them saying, "Receive ye the Holy Ghost."

CHAPTER VI

The Holy Spirit in Conversion

THE HOLY SPIRIT BEGINS THE PROCESS OF CONVERSION

NOW let us interrupt the historical sketch of the ministry of the Holy Spirit and examine the scriptures which set forth the ministry of the Holy Spirit in the conversion of the believer. "When He is come, He will reprove the world." John 16:8. At the very beginning of the salvation process, it is the Holy Spirit who takes the initiative and brings conviction to the sinning heart. "No man can say that Jesus is the Lord, but by the Holy Ghost." 1 Cor. 12:3. Confessing with the mouth is man's first step toward salvation. He yields to the conviction of the Spirit and by the Holy Spirit he calls Jesus Lord.

HE COMPLETES THE PROCESS

A description of what takes place when one is converted is provided by Paul in 2 Thess. 2:13 and by Peter in 1 Peter 1:2. "God hath . . . chosen you to salvation through sanctification of the Spirit and belief of the truth." "Through sanctification of the Spirit, unto obedience and sprinkling of the blood of Jesus Christ." Belief of the truth leads to salvation through the choosing and setting apart of the blessed Holy Spirit. The Spirit lays His Hand of choice upon the sinner's head; the sinner responds by receiving a love of the truth (2 Thess. 2:10) and faith springs up in his heart. God and man co-operate to man's salvation. As Peter describes it, man's part is to obey. "Through sanctification of the Spirit and obedience." This joint work of the Spirit and man results in the sprinkling of the blood of Jesus, which is the indispensable, culminating act of the salvation process. "What can wash away my sin? Nothing but the blood of Jesus." This completed work of the Holy Spirit within the heart of man is called the new birth. Jesus, James, Peter, and John describe it by this term. John 3:5; James 1:18; 1 Peter 1:23; 1 John 3:9; 5:1.

OTHER DESCRIPTIVE TERMS FOR CONVERSION

"God hath sent forth the Spirit of His Son into your hearts, crying, Abba Father." Gal. 4:6. This is a plain statement that the Holy Spirit comes into one's heart at conversion. As a matter of fact, "if any man have not the Spirit of Christ, he is none of His." Roman 8:9. This original salvation experience is also described by Paul as a baptism into the body of Christ. "For by one Spirit are we all baptized into one body." 1 Cor. 12:13. "For as many as have been baptized into Christ have put on Christ." Gal. 3:27. And finally, the Spirit "witnesses" with our spirit "that we are the children of God." Romans 8:16.

ALL BELIEVERS HAVE THE HOLY SPIRIT

In all the descriptions and the use of different terms to explain the conversion of the believer, it is clearly stated that the Holy Spirit is the agent at conversion. He convicts men of sin; He sanctifies or sets them apart unto salvation; and they are born of the Spirit. He witnesses that they are children of God. They who are Christ's have the Spirit of Christ. The Holy Spirit baptizes them into the body of Christ, and the Holy Spirit resides in their hearts. Thus we see that all true born-again believers have the Holy Spirit. They have truly "begun in the Spirit." Gal. 3:3. All that they have in the way of Christian vitality and experience is the work of the Holy Spirit.

JOHN 20:22

We can now understand more clearly what happened to the disciples on the night of the resurrection when Jesus said, "Receive ye the Holy Ghost." This Spirit of the resurrected, glorified Christ was now available for human hearts, and Jesus hastened to impart this life to His disciples. The Spirit of God's Son, the Spirit of Christ, as the Spirit of conversion, came into their hearts on that occasion. He had died and become a glorified being in order that He might come into the lives of all believers. In the words of Matthew Henry's Commentary on this verse, "As the breath of the Almighty gave life to man, and began the old world, so the breath of the Mighty Savior gave life to His ministers, and began the new world."

"With You And Shall Be In You."

There is mystery connected with the fact that the Spirit of Christ was *in* Old Testament prophets (1 Peter 1:11; Neh. 9:30) and *in* New Testament believers (Gal. 4:6), and yet was only *with* the disciples during Christ's earthly ministry. "He dwelleth *with* you and shall be *in* you." John 14:17. This mystery has to do with the relation of the Person of Christ to the Person of the Holy Spirit. The latter is the "other self" of the former and, since Christ was compelled, by the nature of the physical body which He occupied, merely to be *with* them before He was glorified, it was therefore logically true that His Spirit (the Holy Spirit) was also *with* them and not *in* them until Christ rose from the dead. John 20:22 was the first step of the Spirit's incoming. The final fulfillment of John 14:17 came on the day of Pentecost.

We know from what is recorded in St. John's Gospel that even before the ascension, the Holy Ghost had actually been given to the disciples, that Christ breathed upon them the Holy Ghost.

But on the Day of Pentecost they were filled with the Holy Ghost.[1]

---

[1]Hopkin, *Law of Liberty*, p. 205, as quoted in J. Elder Cumming, D.D., *Through the Eternal Spirit* (Drummond Tract Depot, London: 1937), P. 78.

CHAPTER VII

The Baptism in the Holy Spirit Distinguished From Conversion

ALL BELIEVERS MAY BE BAPTIZED IN THE SPIRIT.

IT was shown in the previous chapter that the visitation of the Holy Spirit on the resurrection night was entirely different from the Baptism of the Holy Spirit which came fifty days later. This leads us to the further conclusion that, although all believers have the Holy Spirit, yet it still remains that all believers, in addition to having the Holy Spirit, may be filled with or baptized with the Holy Spirit. As Dr. R. A. Torrey, first head of the Moody Bible Institute, has written:

It is evident that the baptism with the Holy Spirit is an operation of the Holy Spirit distinct from and additional to His regenerating work.

. . . A man may be regenerated by the Holy Spirit and still not be baptized with the Holy Spirit. In regeneration, there is the impartation of life by the Spirit's power, and the one who receives it is saved: in the baptism with the Holy Spirit, there is the impartation of power, and the one who receives it is fitted for service. . . .[1]

Hopkins also says, "We must recognize the fact that to have the Spirit is one thing, but to be filled with the Spirit is quite another thing."[2]

CHRIST'S RELATION TO THE SPIRIT

Jesus was born of the Holy Spirit from the virgin Mary's womb. For thirty years He was the Son of God in a sense that no one else has been. Then at the River Jordan, He was baptized in the Holy Spirit. He received the anointing from on high which launched Him upon and maintained Him in that most dynamic ministry. A. J. Gordon makes the same distinction.

Let us observe that Christ, who is our example in this as in all things, did not appear upon His ministry till he had received the Holy Ghost. . . . He had been begotten of the Holy Ghost in

---

[1]R. A. Torrey, *The Person and Work of the Holy Spirit* (Fleming H. Revell: New York [c. 1910]), pp. 174, 176.
[2]Hopkins, op. cit., p. 205.

the womb of the virgin, and had lived that holy and obedient life which this divine nativity would imply. But when he would enter upon his public ministry, he waited for the Spirit to come upon him, as he had hitherto been in him.[1]

The late eminent English Baptist clergyman, F. B. Meyer, has called attention to Christ's being born of the Spirit and later baptized in the Spirit.

Jesus Christ was conceived of the Holy Ghost, and for thirty years Jesus was led and taught by the divine Spirit. Was He not one with the Holy Ghost? Certainly. Why then must He be anointed? Because His human nature needed to be empowered by the Spirit, before even He could do successful service in this world. Jesus waited for thirty years until He was anointed, and only then did He say, "The Spirit of the Lord is upon me, and he hath anointed me to preach." Never forget that our Lord's ministry was not in the power of the second person of the blessed Trinity, but in the power of the third person.[2]

Dr. A. B. Simpson, godly founder of the Christian and Missionary Alliance, has written as follows:

---

[1] A. J. Gordon, *Ministry of the Spirit* (Fleming H. Revell Company. New York [c. 1894]), p. 75.

[2] F. B. Meyer, *A Castaway*, p. 86.

First, He was born by the Spirit, then He was baptized by the Spirit, and then He went forth to work out His life and ministry in the power of the Spirit. But "He that sanctifieth and they that are sanctified are all of one"; so in like manner we must follow in His footsteps and re-live His life. Born like Him of the Spirit, we, too, must be baptized of the Spirit, and then go forth to live *His* life and reproduce His work.[1]

THE DISCIPLES' RELATION TO THE SPIRIT

The disciples of Christ had left all to follow Him. Matt. 19:27. They had confessed that He was the Christ, the Son of the Living God. Matt. 16:16; John 6:68, 69. Jesus had pronounced them clean (John 15:3) with the exception of Judas. John 13:10, 11. He had also declared that their names were written in heaven. Luke 10:20. Then He had breathed on them the Holy Spirit power after His resurrection. John 20:22. And yet they were commanded to tarry to receive the baptism in the Holy Spirit. Luke 24:49. They had received the Holy Spirit already, but they yet needed the baptism in the Holy Spirit. Andrew Murray says:

---

[1]A. B. Simpson, D.D., *The Holy Spirit, or Power From on High*, Vol. II (Christian Alliance Publishing Co., New York [1924]), p. 21.

To the disciples, the baptism of the Spirit was very distinctly not his first bestowal for regeneration, but the definite communication of his presence in power of their glorified Lord. . . . Just as there was a twofold operation of the one Spirit in the Old and New Testaments, of which the state of the disciples before and after Pentecost was the striking illustration, so there may be, and in the majority of Christians is, a corresponding difference of experience.[1]

THE SAMARITAN CONVERTS' RELATION TO THE SPIRIT

The disciples at Samaria received Christ under the preaching of Philip. Acts 8:5-13. There was great joy in that city. "They believed Philip preaching the things concerning the kingdom of God and the name of Jesus Christ, and were baptized both men and women." v.12. Without any doubt, the Holy Spirit was present in the ministry of Philip. He was a man that was himself full of the Holy Spirit as declared in Acts 6:3, 5. His converts had been won and their regeneration had been effected by the Holy Spirit, for there was no other way.

They Later Received the Holy Spirit

Acts 8:14-17 reads as follows: "Now when the apostles which were at Jerusalem heard that Samaria

---

[1]Andrew Murray, *The Spirit of Christ* (Nisbet & Co., London, 1888), page 323.

had received the Word of God, they sent unto them Peter and John: who when they were come down, prayed for them that they might receive the Holy Ghost: (for as yet he was fallen upon none of them: only they were baptized in the name of the Lord Jesus.) Then laid they their hands on them, and they received the Holy Ghost." It was the baptism of the Holy Spirit which the Samaritan disciples needed and which the apostles at Jerusalem hastened to impart unto them. The Holy Spirit had worked within their hearts and was present there as the Spirit of Christ, but "as yet he was fallen upon none of them."

This Experience More Wonderful Than the Miracles

The power of the Holy Spirit coming upon them through the hands of Peter and John effected such a marvelous result in the lives of these disciples that Simon offered money that this power which Peter and John had might be given to him. He had not offered to buy Philip's evangelistic zeal, nor Philip's gifts of healing, miracles, and faith. But the mighty baptism of the Holy Spirit which came upon the Samaritan disciples was to his mind more spectacular and wonderful. This explains his offer to buy this power and his neglect to offer to buy the previous working of the Holy Spirit. All of this is definite proof that there was a difference between the conversion of the Samaritan disciples and their baptism in the Holy Spirit, also that this baptism in the

Holy Spirit was a most powerful and convincing experience.

PAUL'S RELATION TO THE HOLY SPIRIT

When Paul heard the voice and saw the light from heaven, brighter than the light of the midday sun, he said, "Who art thou, Lord?" and "Lord, what wilt thou have me to do?" He called Jesus "Lord." In the statement of 1 Cor. 12:3, he could not have done this but by the Holy Spirit. This was the moment of his conversion. He acknowledged Him as Lord and surrendered his life completely to his Lord's direction. Upon his arrival at Damascus, Ananias was sent to him and addressed him as "Brother Saul." He was indeed a brother, for he had been converted on the way to Damascus. Ananias laid hands upon him that he might receive his sight and be filled with the Holy Spirit. Thus three days intervened between his conversion and his being filled with the Spirit.

THE EPHESIAN DISCIPLES' RELATION TO THE SPIRIT

In the 19th chapter of Acts, we have the record of the disciples at Ephesus who had been baptized unto the baptism of John and who were asked by Paul if they had received the Holy Spirit since, or when, they believed. Both the main verb in this sentence and the participial form properly translated "when you believed" are in the Greek aorist tense which indicate action in past time. The participle might be rendered "having believed," which would distinguish between the receiving of the Holy Spirit (in baptismal fullness) and the original believing in Christ unto salvation. But what is the significance of Paul's question? If all disciples receive this experience of the Holy Spirit when they believe, why did Paul ask these disciples if they had done so? His very question implies that it is possible to believe without receiving the fullness of the Holy Spirit. In the words of A. J. Gordon, "This passage (Acts 19:2) seems decisive as showing that one may be a disciple without having entered into possession of the Spirit as God's gift to believers."[1]

The same distinction is made in Eph. 1:13, referring to the experience recorded in Acts 19.

They Believe and Then Receive the Spirit

After having explained to them concerning Christ, they were baptized again, this time not unto John's baptism but unto Christ's. After they accepted Christ and were baptized in His name, Paul laid his hands upon them, the Holy Spirit came upon them, and they spoke with tongues and prophesied. Surely no one would claim that one should be baptized in water before conversion. Thus the Ephesian disciples were converted to Christ, then baptized in water, and then received the Holy Spirit. This whole passage

---

[1]A. J. Gordon, *The Ministry of the Spirit,* (Fleming H. Revell Company, New York [c. 1894]), page 71.

very clearly sets forth the difference between believing in Christ and receiving the Holy Spirit with prophesying.

RELATION OF THE CONVERTS ON THE DAY OF PENTECOST TO THE HOLY SPIRIT

When Peter preached on the day of Pentecost, he instructed his audience to repent and be baptized, saying that they then would receive the gift of the Holy Spirit. The Holy Spirit had pricked their hearts. At their repentance He would baptize them into the Body of Christ. Then they would take a public stand for Christ by being baptized in water in His name. Following that, they would receive the gift of the Holy Spirit. Referring to Acts 2:38, Rev. A. J. Gordon says: "This passage shows logically and chronologically the gift of the Spirit is subsequent to repentance."[1]

William Kelley says:

Therefore it is evident that the reception of the Holy Ghost, as here spoken of, has nothing whatever to do with bringing men to believe and repent. It is a subsequent operation; it is an additional and separate blessing; it is a privilege founded on faith already actively working in the heart. . . . I do not mean to deny that the gift of the Holy Ghost may be practically on the same occasion, but never in the same moment. The

---

[1]Ibid., p. 69.

reason is quite simple too. The gift of the Holy
Ghost is grounded on the fact that we are sons by
faith in Christ, believers resting on redemption in
him. Plainly therefore, it appears that the Spirit
of God has already regenerated us.[1]

FEASTS OF PASSOVER AND PENTECOST AS TYPES

In the establishment of the Feast of Pentecost in
the beginning, its date was placed fifty days after
the Passover and the Feast of the Sheaf of the
First-fruits. Without the Passover, the day of Pentecost could not have been determined or have come.
This is true also of that which these feasts typify.
First, Christ our Passover; and then, the Holy
Spirit at Pentecost. How significant that the jubila-
tion of Pentecost should come on the Jubilee Day
following the Passover!

THE BLOOD AND THE OIL AS TYPES

Also in the cleansing of the leper, the blood was
first placed "upon the tip of the right ear of him
that is to be cleansed, and upon the thumb of his
right hand, and upon the great toe of his right
foot." And then the oil was put on the places where

---

[1]William Kelley, *Lectures on the New Testament Doctrine
of the Holy Spirit*, p. 161, as quoted in A. J. Gordon, *The
Ministry of the Spirit*, (Fleming H. Revell, New York, [c.
1894]), pp. 69, 70.

the blood had been applied. Lev. 14:14-17. The oil upon the blood shows that we must have the blood of Jesus applied to our hearts before we receive the Spirit's work in our lives. If this oil represents the Spirit's work at conversion, which it doubtless does, the type has more to teach us. "And the remnant of the oil that is in the priest's hand, he shall pour upon the head of him that is to be cleansed." v.18. This typifies the anointing of the Holy Spirit which comes at the Baptism in the Spirit.

THE OIL IN AND UPON THE MEAL OFFERING AS A TYPE

In the meal offering of Leviticus 2, the same truth is taught. "And if the oblation be a meat offering baken in a pan, it shall be of fine flour mingled with oil. Thou shalt part it in pieces, and pour oil thereon: it is a meat-offering." vv. 5, 6. Oil in the cake (the Holy Spirit at conversion), and oil poured upon it (the Holy Spirit at the Baptism).

1 CORINTHIANS 12:13

It is claimed by some that this passage declares that all who are in the body of Christ are thereby, and by the same act, baptized in the Holy Spirit. That this conclusion is wrong is shown by the broadbased argument of all that has been written above. One should compare scripture with scripture in order to get the full, true teaching of the Scripture. This

Scripture-wide teaching that the Holy Spirit baptizes into the body of Christ at conversion and that 1 Cor. 12:13 refers to this experience is stated by John MacNeil as follows:

When Paul declares in 1 Cor. 12:13, "For by one Spirit are we all baptized into one body," he is speaking of every believer having been quickened from the dead by the agency of the Holy Ghost, and thus made a member of Christ's mystical body. This is the Pauline way of stating the being born again of John 3:7.[1]

A BETTER EXEGESIS OF THIS PASSAGE

To claim that 1 Cor. 12:13 teaches that all believers are baptized in the Holy Spirit seems to be faulty exegesis too. "For by one Spirit [literally, in one Spirit, i.e., in virtue of His operation[2]] are we all baptized into one body, whether we be Jews or Gentiles, whether we be bond or free; and have all been made to drink into one Spirit." This is a statement that *by* the Spirit we are baptized into the body of Christ. As water is the element into which the minister baptizes the candidate, so the Body of Christ is the element into which the Holy Spirit baptizes the believer. This does not refer to water baptism but to that of which water baptism is a symbol. The use of the word "baptize" in this connection is unique. Eph. 4:5 reads: "There is

---

[1]John MacNeil, *Spirit-Filled Life*, p. 38.
[2]Cambridge Greek Testament.

one Lord, one faith, one baptism." Yet the Bible mentions at least four baptisms: in water, in the Spirit, in the Body of Christ, and in suffering. Only one of these (that in water) is physical: the others are spiritual; and the word "baptism" in connection with these other elements is a figure of speech. *Like as* a minister baptizes in water, so the Spirit is the Agent (by, "en") who takes a person and baptizes, buries, builds, engrafts (to use different figures) or places him (to be literal) in the Body of Christ. This is simply and only a reference to what takes place at conversion as described in the last chapter. The last clause of 1 Cor. 12:13, "and have all been made to drink into one Spirit," may refer to the Baptism in the Spirit. The Corinthians had been baptized into the Body of Christ, and also into the Holy Spirit. The two clauses of this verse, then, speak of two experiences: salvation, and the Baptism in the Spirit.

STATEMENTS BY TORREY, CUMMING, AND MURRAY

Dr. R. A. Torrey sums up his discussion concerning this matter thus:

"So it is as clear as language can possibly make it, that it is one thing to be born again and something further, something additional, to be baptized with the Holy Spirit. It is clear and undeniable, therefore, that one may be a regenerate man and not as yet have received the Baptism with the Holy Spirit. Let us bow to the clear teaching of the Word of God even if it does not agree with our preconceived theories.[1]

It seems to me beyond question, as a matter of experience, both of Christians in the present day, and of the early church as recorded by inspiration, that in addition to the gift of the Spirit received at conversion, there is another blessing, corresponding in its signs and effects to the blessing received by the Apostles at Pentecost; a blessing to be asked for and expected by Christians still, and to be described in language similar to that employed in the book of Acts.[2]

To the disciples, the Baptism of the Spirit was very distinctly not his first bestowal for regeneration, but the definite communication of his presence in power of their glorified Lord. Just as there was a twofold operation of the one Spirit in the Old and New Testaments, of which the state of the disciples before and after Pentecost was the striking illustration, so there may be, and in the majority of Christians is, a correspond-

---

[1]R. A. Torrey, *The Holy Spirit, Who He Is, What He Does*, p. 114, as quoted in Elmer C. Miller, *Pentecost Examined* (Gospel Publishing House, Springfield, Mo. [c. 1936]), p. 29.
[2]J. Elder Cumming, D.D., *Through the Eternal Spirit* (London: Drummond Tract Depot, 1937), p. 83.

ing difference of experience. . . . When once the distinct recognition of what the indwelling of the Spirit was meant to bring is brought home to the soul, . . . the believer may ask and expect what may be termed a baptism of the Spirit. Praying to the Father, . . . he may receive such an inflow of the Holy Spirit as shall consciously lift him to a different level from the one on which he had hitherto lived. . . . The desire is growing among God's people to have nothing less than what God meant by His promise of a baptism with the Holy Ghost and with fire.[8]

SUMMARY AND CONFIRMATION

By way of summary, there are six Scriptural examples of the difference between salvation by the power of the Holy Spirit and the Baptism in the Spirit: Christ, His disciples, the Samaritans, Paul, the Ephesians, and the converts on the day of Pentecost. There are three Old Testament pictures of this distinction: the Feasts of Passover and Pentecost, the cleansing of the leper, and the meal offering. It is confirmed by the two clauses of 1 Cor. 12:13; by John 14:17 (the Comforter, *"whom the world cannot receive"*); by Acts 19:2 ("Have ye received the Holy Ghost *since* (or when) ye believed?"); and by Eph. 1:13 (*"after* that ye believed, ye were sealed with that Holy Spirit of promise").

----

[8]Andrew Murray, *The Spirit of Christ* (Nisbet & Co., London [c. 1888]), pp. 323-325.

CHAPTER VIII

The Baptism in the Holy Spirit, Distinctive Names and Description

SALVATION DESCRIBED BY DIFFERENT TERMS

THE initial experience of salvation is described in the Bible by different terms. "Ye must be born again." John 3:3. "Except ye be converted." Matt. 18:3. "He that believeth and is baptized shall be saved." Mark 16:16. "If any man hear my voice and open the door, I will come in to him." Rev. 3:21. The new birth, conversion, salvation, and letting Jesus come into our heart, all mean the same thing and refer to that wonderful experience which we have when we first get right with God.

THE SPIRIT'S COMING LIKEWISE DESCRIBED

In like manner that glorious experience which is subsequent to salvation and distinct from the initial contact with God is also referred to and described by many names in the Holy Scripture. "Ye shall be *baptized* with the Holy Ghost not many days hence." Acts 1:5. "They were all *filled* with the Holy Ghost." Acts 2:4. "Ye shall *receive the gift* of the Holy Ghost." Acts 2:38. "The Holy Ghost *fell on* them." Acts 10:44. "He which hath *anointed* us is God, who hath also *sealed* us and given us the *earnest* of the Spirit in our hearts." 2 Cor. 1:21-22. Thus we have seven distinct terms which are used in connection with this glorious experience which is promised to believers subsequent to salvation.

DIFFERENT TERMS FOR ONE EXPERIENCE

It must not be considered that these different terms refer to different experiences. When John Baptist and Jesus referred to the advent of the Spirit as being baptized in the Spirit (Matt. 3:11; Acts 1:5), their reference was to the day of Pentecost when "they were all *filled with* the Holy Ghost." Acts 2:4. When the Holy Ghost *fell* on the household of Cornelius, *"as on us at the beginning,"* Peter remembered "the word of the Lord, how that he said, . . . Ye shall be *baptized* with the Holy Ghost." Acts 11:15, 16. The Holy Spirit had not *fallen* on the converts at Samaria until Peter and John prayed for them and they *received* the Holy Ghost. Acts 8:16, 17. Thus *baptize, fill, fall on,* and *receive* are synonymous terms referring to one and the same experience. But there is a significance in using the different terms, as we shall see.

RECEIVING THE SPIRIT

Notice first of all the expression, "receiving the gift of the Holy Ghost." This phrase occurs eleven times in the New Testament. It was used by Peter on the day of Pentecost in his assurance to his audience that they too might receive the same wonderful experience which the 120 disciples had just received. In the 8th chapter of Acts it is recorded that Peter and John came down to Samaria and prayed for them that they might *receive* the Holy Ghost. "Then laid they their hands on them, and they *received* the Holy Ghost. And when Simon saw that through the laying on of the apostles' hands *the Holy Ghost was given,* he offered them money, saying, Give me also this power that on whomsoever I lay hands he may receive the Holy Ghost." Paul asked the Ephesians, "Have ye *received* the Holy Ghost since ye believed?" Acts 19:2. All of these scriptures emphasize the fact that this glorious experience is a gift from Heaven and is to be had by simple receiving on our part. Paul said in Gal. 3:14, "that we might *receive* the promise of the Spirit through faith"—*not* by works of righteousness which we have done; *not* by our own holiness or merit; *not* as a reward for any fasting and prayer; *not* as payment to us in any way whatsoever; but as a sheer gift of His infinite grace and love. He is offered to us freely without money and without price. We merely extend our hand of faith, lay hold on Him, appropriate Him, and receive Him as our own.

FALLING ON THEM

In Peter's sermon he referred to the experience which they had just received as that which the Lord Jesus had received of the Father and *had shed* forth upon them. In the Samaritan experience, the Holy Record reads: "for as yet He was *fallen upon* none of them." Down at Cornelius' household, "while Peter yet spake these words, the Holy Ghost *fell on* all them which heard the word." Acts 10:44. Again at Ephesus, "when Paul had laid his hands upon them the Holy Ghost *came upon* them." Acts 19:6. Such expressions indicate a descent of the Holy Ghost from heaven. They occur ten times in all. He comes as a mighty torrent, being poured out upon waiting believers. He falls upon them. He comes upon them as dew from on high. How descriptive and realistic these terms are! How graphically they described this wonderful experience! Upon some He settles down as heavenly dew, and they sweetly and quietly speak forth in other tongues. This is the refreshing wherewith He will cause the weary to rest. Isa. 28:11, 12. Upon others He falls as if the very sky were coming down upon them. They are overwhelmed with the impact of His coming and many times fall prostrate under His power. This is all indicated by the terms which are used to describe His descent upon them. It is very real and true to experience.

THE FIGURE OF BAPTISM

John the Baptist said, "I indeed baptize you with water. But one mightier than I cometh, the latchet of whose shoes I am not worthy to unloose; He shall baptize you with the Holy Ghost and with fire." Luke 3:16. This figure of baptism is used six times in the New Testament with reference to this additional experience. When a minister baptizes in water, he takes the candidate and submerges him completely out of sight under the water. There must be a perfect yieldedness on the part of the candidate for baptism. Co-operation by active participation does not assist, but rather hinders the one who is baptizing. There must be complete relaxation and surrender into the control of the individual who is baptizing. Baptism is submersion and is not complete until every portion of the body of the one baptized is completely out of sight under the water. He is then raised up and comes out of the water, literally drenched and dripping with the element in which he was baptized. He emerges, as one who has been baptized, having entered once for all into this new state.

The Figure Applied.

All of this is accurately typical and a graphic picture of the experience appropriately called the baptism with the Holy Spirit. Jesus is the minister who officiates at this baptism in the Holy Spirit. We present our whole being to Him. Body, soul, and spirit must be yielded. Our physical bodies must be pliable under His power. The tongue is the most unruly of the human members, and the complete abandonment of that tongue to the control of the Holy Spirit indicates that the entire being is surrendered unto Him. Thus yielded to our Christ, we are taken into His wonderful charge and submerged into the great Spiritual Element which is none other than the actual Person of the Holy Spirit. This baptism is not complete until every part of one's spirit is saturated and permeated by the blessed Holy Spirit. We come forth, having been baptized in the Spirit, living now continually in this new state.

Almost Baptized.

There are many spiritual experiences which approximate the baptism in the Holy Spirit. As Ezekiel's river was first ankle deep, then knee deep, then loin deep, and finally waters to swim in; so there are various degrees to which one can "wade out" into the blessed Holy Spirit. Utter and complete baptism in the Holy Spirit, however, is reached only when there is a perfect yielding of the entire being to Him and one's tongue is surrendered to the control of the blessed Holy Spirit. As one passes into this experience, he becomes drenched and dripping with the power of Almighty God. How very accurate is this description of the Holy Spirit's coming conveyed to us by the figure of baptism!

The Figure of Baptism in a Cloud.

This figure of water baptism can be amplified somewhat and still remain in Scriptural bounds. Paul said (1 Cor. 10:1,2) that "all our fathers were under the cloud, and all passed through the sea; and were all baptized unto Moses in the cloud and in the sea." This was typical of the experience which children of God have today. They escape from Egypt (the world) by virtue of Christ our Passover being sacrificed for them (1 Cor. 5:7); then they pass through the waters of baptism (Mark 16:16), typified by the waters of the Red Sea. What does being "baptized in the cloud" typify? We answer, the Baptism in the Holy Spirit. That cloud was the Shekinah glory of Almighty God. It was a cloud by day and a pillar of fire by night. It not only represented God but it was God in His continuous presence. "And *the Lord* went before them by day *in* a pillar of a cloud to lead them the way; and by night *in* a pillar of fire to give them light; to go by day and night." Ex. 13:21. He hung low over His people and they literally walked in that cloud, being surrounded by God Himself. This was a continuing experience for them through their entire wilderness journey. Num. 9:15-23.

This Figure Applied.

This figure of baptism into a cloud, which is

a continuing in the element into which we have been baptized, is an appropriate picture of the Baptism in the Holy Spirit. We do not go into and then quickly out of, as in water baptism, but we go into and remain in, as in a heavenly cloud. By this experience we enter into the Holy Spirit and live on and walk on with the Shekinah glory of God surrounding us. This glorious Presence proceeds onward and we proceed with Him. We remain enveloped in this cloud, continually walking on with God. This element in which we remain baptized is a Spirit Person, a Divine Person, the Third Person in the Holy Trinity. We are actually *in* the Spirit. "Ye are not in the flesh, but *in the Spirit,* if so be that the Spirit of God dwell in you." Rom. 8:9. "If we live *in the Spirit,* let us also walk *in the Spirit.*" Gal. 5:25. It is a state of being in constant contact with and enveloped by this Person now and forevermore.

FILLED

In describing this experience, the Divine Author also uses the expression, "they were all filled with the Holy Ghost." Acts 2:4. This represents not merely a receiving of the Spirit or a being baptized into Him but a condition and a state of becoming filled and remaining filled with this Divine Power. Peter was still filled with the Holy Spirit as he made his defense before the Sanhedrin. Acts 4:8. The deacons who were chosen were men full of the Holy Spirit. Acts 6:3, 5. Stephen in his martyrdom was likewise full of the Holy Spirit. Acts 7:55. Paul was not only filled with the Holy Spirit by the laying on of the hands of Ananias at Damascus, but he remained full of the Holy Spirit in his missionary ministry. Acts 13:9. This is also a true description of this experience into which the Lord would bring us subsequent to original conversion.

CHAPTER IX

Baptism in the Holy Spirit, Symbols Describing It

ANOINTING

THE baptism in the Holy Spirit is sometimes referred to as an *anointing.* 2 Cor. 1:21; 1 John 2:27; Acts 10:38. To the Jewish mind and to one familiar with Old Testament practice, an anointing represents a divine dedication and a consecration to a holy office. As Aaron and his sons were inducted into the priesthood, a holy ointment was prepared and used for their anointing. This anointing was their consecration into the priest's office. Ex. 30:30; Lev. 8:12. As choice was to be made in Israel of the first king, God instructed Samuel, who found Saul, took a vial of oil, and poured it over his head. 1 Sam. 10:1 A few years later as Saul was rejected and David was chosen to be his successor, "Samuel took the horn of oil and anointed him in the midst of his brethren, and the

Spirit of the Lord came upon David from that day forward." 1 Sam. 16:13. As Elijah approached the hour of the conclusion of his ministry, he was instructed by the Lord to anoint Elisha, the son of Shaphat, to be his successor. 1 Kings 19:16. From these Scriptures we see that prophet, priest, and king were all anointed as an official indication of their choice and dedication to their respective offices.

Jesus' Anointing.

As Jesus, the great antitype of prophet, priest and king, stood up to preach in Nazareth, He said, "The Spirit of the Lord is upon me, because He hath anointed me," etc. Luke 4:18. The anointing which came upon our Great Head was "like the precious ointment upon the head, that ran down upon the beard, even Aaron's beard: that went down to the skirts of his garments." Psa. 133:2. The anointing which came on Christ flows down to the remotest member of His body who will accept the precious ointment.

Our Anointing.

They who receive this joyous experience should realize that they have been consecrated and dedicated by the Almighty God Himself to distinctive office and ministry. As prophets we are anointed to preach, teach, and tell the good news. As priests we are anointed to make intercession for all men. As kings we are anointed to reign in life now and to share the throne with Jesus Christ our Lord. Truly this great anointing with the Holy Spirit is a most significant experience.

SEALING

To be *sealed* with the Holy Spirit (2 Cor. 1:22; Eph. 1:13; and 4:30) is to have Him come upon us in the capacity of shutting us in with God. He constitutes a seal between us and the world. As the housewife seals her canned fruit that outside air may not penetrate and it remains preserved as long as the seal is not broken, so our lives are covered over with the Holy Spirit seal to keep out the evil influences of this impure world. As long as this seal remains unbroken, we are preserved blameless in spirit, soul, and body unto the coming of our Lord Jesus Christ. 1 Thess. 5:23. When Jesus was buried, the chief priests made the sepulchre sure, sealing the stone, and setting a watch. Matt. 27:66. This was doubtless the seal of the government and indicated its authority. To tamper with that seal was an attack on the government itself. The seal of official documents today carries the authority of the institution issuing the document. From this we gather that he who touches us attacks the great government which has endorsed us. Also a seal or a brand is often stamped upon an article or upon cattle to indicate certain ownership.

Christ's Sealing and Ours.

Jesus, our Head and Example, was sealed by God the Father. John 6:27.

[73]

If we can learn aright how Christ was sealed, we shall learn how we are sealed. The sealing of Christ by the Father is the communication of the Holy Spirit in fullness to Him, authorizing Him unto and acting His divine power in all the acts and duties of His office, so as to evidence the presence of God with Him and approbation of Him. God's sealing of believers then is His gracious communication of the Holy Spirit unto them so as to act His divine power in them as to enable them unto all the duties of their holy calling, evidencing them to be accepted with Him both for themselves and others, and asserting their preservation unto eternal life.[1]

"The foundation of God standeth sure, having this seal, the Lord knoweth them that are His: and let every one that nameth the name of Christ depart from iniquity." 2 Tim. 2:19. Here both ideas of ownership and preservation from evil are indicated by the seal. The duration of this seal is until the day of redemption. Eph. 4:30. Thereafter His protection will not be needed, since we will be in the presence of God Himself, removed from all danger of corruption and attack.

AN EARNEST

Three times in the New Testament (2 Cor. 1:22;

---

[1]John Owen, D.D., *Discourse Concerning the Spirit*, pp. 406, 407, as quoted in A. J. Gordon, *The Ministry of the Spirit* (Fleming H. Revell, New York 1894), p. 82

5:5; and Eph. 1:14), it is stated that the experience of the Holy Spirit coming upon us is the *earnest* of our inheritance. This is a reference to the Old Testament practice of receiving a very small portion of that which has been purchased or promised as a token and pledge that the full purchase will be delivered in due time. By this means it is indicated to us that this glorious experience, which we usually call the Baptism in the Holy Spirit, is but a sample and a foretaste of that effulgence of glory which will be ours at the coming of our Lord.

OTHER SYMBOLS OF THE HOLY SPIRIT

In addition to oil, a seal, and an earnest, there are a few other symbols which are used with reference to the Holy Spirit. It is not specifically recorded that they have to do with the operation of the Holy Spirit as He comes in fullness upon the believer, but they are symbols of the Person of the Holy Spirit in whatever capacity He manifests Himself upon earth. But since they represent characteristics of the Holy Spirit, we may expect them to be most manifest when the believer is baptized with the Holy Spirit.

Fire.

One of these symbols is fire. The children of Israel were preceded through the wilderness by a pillar of cloud by day and a pillar of fire by night. Ex. 13:21, 22. John the Baptist said, "He shall baptize you with the Holy Ghost and with fire. . . .

[75]

He will thoroughly purge his floor and . . . burn up the chaff with unquenchable fire." Matt. 3:11, 12; Luke 3:16, 17. On the day of Pentecost tongues like as of fire sat upon each of them. Acts 2:3. Our God is a consuming fire. Heb. 12:29. Nothing less than fire can picture to us the consuming holiness of our God. All dross and impurities are burned out by His purging presence, and the soul is set afire with a flaming zeal and burning passion for God and His service. Also the fire of persecution awaits those who yield themselves to this baptism. Christ was driven immediately into the wilderness to be tempted of the devil. The apostles shortly after Pentecost were thrown into prison. And today the reproach of Pentecost is still a fire that burns. But why should we fear the fire when He will be with us in the flame?

Wind.

Jesus said to Nicodemus, "the wind bloweth where it listeth, and thou hearest the sound thereof, but canst not tell whence it cometh, and whither it goeth: so is everyone that is born of the Spirit." John 3:8. The very word "pneuma" which, as it refers to the Holy Spirit, is translated "spirit," is in reality the ordinary Greek word for "wind" or "air." Jehovah *breathed* upon Adam and he became a living soul. Christ *breathed* upon His disciples and said, "Receive ye the Holy Ghost." John 20:22. The Spirit was His very breath or life. On the day of Pentecost there came a sound from Heaven as of a rushing mighty wind, and it filled all the house where they were sitting; and they were all filled with the Holy Ghost. The Holy Spirit is around us constantly and is everywhere, as the very air we breathe. He is our very life in God. When the air moves, a delightful breeze is the result. When the Holy Spirit moves specially, as He did upon the prophets of old, He is represented as a wind. He comes as a great torrent of air and fills waiting believers.

Water.

To the woman at the Samaritan well, Jesus used the figure of water. "But whosoever drinketh of the water that I shall give him shall never thirst; but the water that I shall give him shall be in him a well of water springing up into everlasting life." "God is a Spirit and they that worship Him must worship him in Spirit and in truth." John 4:14, 24. On the last day of the feast, He cried, "If any man thirst, let him come unto Me and drink. He that believeth on Me, as the Scripture hath said, out of his belly shall flow rivers of living water. But this spake He of the Spirit." John 7:37-39. "For I will pour water upon him that is thirsty, and floods upon the dry ground; I will pour my spirit upon thy seed, and my blessing upon thine offspring." Isa. 44:3. Water is absolutely essential to all physical life. Water washes, and so does the Holy Spirit. It refreshes, and so does He. The Holy Spirit is represented in the eternal state as the River of

Life that flows out from under the throne of God and of the Lamb, the Life of the heavenly city. He is the River of Life now to thirsty souls.

Rain and Dew.

As He is distilled from heaven, He is likened unto rain and dew. "He shall come down like rain upon the mown grass." Ps. 72:6. "As the dew of Hermon, and as the dew that descended upon the mountains of Zion." Ps. 133:3. "He shall come unto us as the rain, as the latter and former rain unto the earth." Hosea 6:3. "I will be as the dew unto Israel." Hosea 14:5. "For with stammering lips and another tongue will he speak unto this people. To whom he said, This is the rest wherewith ye may cause the weary to rest; and this is the refreshing." Isa. 28:11, 12. How gently and refreshingly He descends upon the soul, and how life-giving is His coming!

Dove.

John saw the Holy Spirit like a dove descending and remaining upon Him. John 1:32. Tender, gentle, pure, and harmless. Like a dove, the Holy Spirit is easily frightened or grieved. And as the dove is a universal symbol of peace, so the Holy Spirit is God's agent to bring peace to the human heart. A very fitting simile for the blessed Holy Spirit.

CHAPTER X

The Baptism in the Holy Spirit—Its Nature and Importance

THE COMING OF THE HOLY SPIRIT

FROM the evidence present-
ed in preceding chapters, we are now prepared to present a definition and description of the Baptism in
the Holy Spirit which will set forth its nature and
its importance.

This experience marks the coming of the Holy
Spirit into one's life as a Person in His own name
and right. As the Spirit of Christ, He had come at
conversion, imparting the Christ-life, revealing
Christ, and making Him real. At the Baptism in the
Spirit, He Himself in His own person comes upon
and fills the waiting believer. This experience is
as distinct from conversion as the Holy Spirit is

distinct from Christ. His coming to the believer at the Baptism is the coming of the Third Person of the Trinity, in addition to the coming of Christ, which takes place at conversion. This is a part of "so great salvation" and is God's definite gift offered to men. Why accept only part of that which God has provided and promised?

THE COMING OF POWER FROM ON HIGH

This Baptism in the Spirit is the fulfillment of the promise of the Father which endues men with power from on high. Luke 24:49. This is the *sine qua non* of Christian service. They were not to depart out of Jerusalem until they had received this experience. As glorious as was the good news of salvation just wrought by the substitutionary death of Christ on the cross and as urgent as was the need of the proclamation of that Gospel, yet they were not even to attempt preaching one sermon or give one testimony until they received this power with which to preach and to testify. "Ye shall receive power, after that the Holy Ghost is come upon you: and ye shall be witnesses unto me." Acts 1:8. Power first, and then witnessing. "Power to witness" is this mighty Baptism in the Spirit. Why should we presume today to go out and work without His strength? to go out to witness without this power? Dr. Jonathan Goforth, that truly great missionary of the Canadian Presbyterian Church, wrote as follows:

[80]

The Lord Himself met and foiled Satan after first being filled with the Spirit. And no child of God has ever been victorious over the adversary unless empowered from the same source. Our Lord did not permit His chosen followers to witness a word in His name until endued with power from on high. It is true that before that day they were the 'born-again' children of the Father and had the witness of the Spirit. But they were not the Lord's efficient co-workers and never could be until Spirit-filled. This divine empowering is for us as for them. We, too, may do the works which our Lord did, yea, and the greater works.[1]

THE COMING OF OUR HEAD AND LEADER

Without Christ, His disciples were as orphans. John 14:18. Without the Holy Spirit, we are as orphans. He is our ordained Head and Leader. "It seemeth good to the Holy Ghost, and to us." Acts 15:28. "The Holy Ghost said, Separate me Barnabas and Saul for the work whereunto I have called them." Acts 13:2. "They were forbidden of the Holy Ghost to preach the Word in Asia." Acts 16:6. He was, and was ever meant to be, the Personal Leader and Commander of the Church. How can we live and function effectively without our God-

---

[1]Jonathan Goforth, *By My Spirit*, p. 12, as quoted by Elmer C. Miller, *Pentecost Examined* (Gospel Publishing House, Springfield, Mo., 1936), p. 43.

appointed Head and Leader? How disrupting and defeating to the plan and the purpose of God if we do not co-operate at the outset of our Christian experience by receiving the fullness of the Holy Spirit Baptism!

THE COMING OF DIVINE EQUIPMENT

Jesus began His ministry and His miracles after He was baptized in the Holy Spirit. Acts 10:38. Peter was a transformed man on the day of Pentecost. The gifts of God now rested upon him and the other disciples. Tongues, prophecy, healing, faith, miracles, and great boldness and wisdom with which to preach His word were their daily equipment and power. As the varied implements of modern warfare were powerful in the hands of trained soldiers and enabled them to conquer in battle, so God has all this equipment in the Holy Spirit for His warriors. "Wherefore put on the whole armor of God, that ye may be able to stand against the wiles of the devil." Eph. 6:11. Why neglect this splendid, effective equipment which God has provided, and rush headlong as unprepared, unarmed troops into battle?

ITS IMPORTANCE

The importance and need of our receiving the Baptism in the Spirit shortly after conversion is shown by the following:

1. God has provided it.
2. Jesus Himself received it.

3. He commanded His disciples not to proceed without it.

4. All His disciples did receive it, as well as His mother and His brethren.

5. It effected the conversion of 3,000 on the day of Pentecost.

6. It enabled the apostles to fill Jerusalem with their doctrine.

7. It enabled them to perform supernatural signs and wonders.

8. It enabled them to carry the Gospel to every creature of their generation. Col. 1:23.

9. They were careful to lead their converts into the same place of power. Acts 8:14, 15, etc.

10. Christ commands all believers to be filled with the Spirit. Matt. 28:20; Eph. 5:18.

For these reasons, we declare, no Christian should neglect to receive the Baptism in the Holy Spirit.

CHAPTER XI

The Baptism in the Holy Spirit, the Initial Physical Evidence

NEED FOR AN EVIDENCE

THE fruits and results of the Baptism of the Holy Spirit have been described in the previous chapter. A life of intimacy with God and a walk of power in the Spirit are the best proofs that one is filled with the Holy Spirit. The matter which is before us now is the consideration of the initial experience of receiving the Baptism and that outward physical sign which is the evidence of this experience. The Spirit-filled realm and life is so exceedingly important for the Christian that God has arranged it so that one can know very definitely whether or not he has entered into this experience. There is no mere "hope so" or need of being deceived in the matter, for God has given a physical and an audible proof of one's having received the Baptism in the Holy Spirit.

PROPHECY THE EVIDENCE BEFORE PENTECOST

Before the day of Pentecost, the people of God constituted a nation. The door was open to others to join that nation, but anyone seeking salvation would have to become circumcised and thus become a Jew. In the words of Christ, "salvation is of the Jews." John 4:22. Of course this nation had its language, and one language was sufficient then in which to converse with God's people. Thus it happened that when men received the mighty anointing from on high, that experience was evidenced by prophecy. Prophecy is speaking one's own language in the power of the Spirit.

INSTANCES OF PROPHECY

When the seventy elders received of the spirit of Moses they *prophesied*. Numbers 11:25. When the Holy Spirit came upon Saul, the first king of Israel, he *prophesied*. 1 Samuel 10:10. Hence the proverb, "Is Saul also among the prophets?" The prophets, among whom he was, themselves *prophesied*. 1 Samuel 10:5; 19:20. When the Holy Spirit came upon prophets of old, they *"spake as they were moved by the Holy Ghost."* 2 Peter 1:21. Joel *prophesied* that the time would come when God would pour out His Spirit upon all flesh, and they would *proph-*

esy. Joel 2:28, 29. When Elisabeth and Zacharias, the parents of John the Baptist, were filled with the Holy Spirit they, too, *prophesied* wonderful words in the Spirit. Luke 1:41, 42, 67. Thus we see that prophecy was the evidence or sign of the reception of the Holy Spirit's power before the day of Pentecost.

TONGUES THE EVIDENCE AT PENTECOST

Now at the beginning of the church dispensation, the field of operation for gospel ministry was widened to include all nations. Jesus had said, "Go into all the world and preach the Gospel." "Go ye therefore and teach all nations." The power of the Holy Ghost was to enable them to witness both at Jerusalem, Judea, Samaria, and the uttermost parts of the earth. The disciples were instructed to wait until they received power from on high before beginning this world-wide ministry. It was very fitting then that instead of the *mother* tongue in prophecy being used as an evidence of the reception of the Holy Ghost, in the church dispensation there should come a divine power which could enable them to speak in *other* tongues, many and varied. On the day of Pentecost there were about fifteen different nationalities present. Among the 120 disciples who were all filled with the Holy Ghost and spoke in other tongues, all fifteen languages were spoken and understood by these nationals who were present. "How hear we every man in our own tongue wherein we were born?" Acts 2:8.

TONGUES ARE CONTINUATION OF PROPHECY AS EVIDENCE

This speaking in other tongues then became the sign and evidence that the Holy Spirit had descended upon New Testament Christians. As a matter of fact, Peter considered that this speaking in other tongues was in reality prophesying. He said, "This is that which was spoken by the prophet Joel. And it shall come to pass in the last days, saith God, I will pour out of my Spirit upon all flesh: and your sons and your daughters shall prophesy, and your young men shall see visions, and your old men shall dream dreams, and on my servants and on my handmaidens I will pour out in those days of my Spirit; and they shall prophesy." Acts 2:16-18. In reality, we are told in 1 Cor. 14:5 that tongues and interpretation are the equivalent of prophecy. As prophecy was the evidence of the baptism when the church or people of God was national, so tongues is the evidence while the church is international.

THE EVIDENCE AT CORNELIUS' HOUSEHOLD

Confirmation of this conclusion is found in the experience of the Gentiles that had gathered together at Cornelius' household. "While Peter yet spake unto them the Holy Ghost fell on all them that heard the Word, and they of the circumcision which believed were astonished, as many as came with Peter, because that on the Gentiles also was

[87]

poured out the gift of the Holy Ghost; for they *heard them speak with tongues* and magnify God." Acts 10:44-46. This was the introduction of this Holy Spirit experience to the Gentiles, and its introduction was evidenced in the very same way as was its coming upon the Jews on the day of Pentecost.

THE EVIDENCE IN THE EXPERIENCE OF PAUL, THE EPHESIANS AND THE CORINTHIANS

It cannot be said that this evidence of tongues was manifest only at the initial outpouring of the Spirit upon the Jews and the Gentiles. Paul was a Jew and was filled with the Holy Spirit and said, "I thank my God I speak with tongues more than ye all." 1 Cor. 14:18. The Gentiles at Ephesus likewise received the Holy Spirit and "spake with tongues and prophesied." Acts 19:6. The Gentiles at Corinth also received this same experience with the speaking in other tongues, for the 12th, 13th and 14th chapters of First Corinthians reveal this fact.

TONGUES THE EVIDENCE TODAY

It is thus manifest that the initial physical evidence of the baptism of the Holy Spirit is the speaking in other tongues as the Spirit gives utterance. On the day of Pentecost "they were *all* filled with the Holy Ghost and began to speak with other tongues as the Spirit gave utterance." At Cornelius' household, "the Holy Ghost fell on *all* them that heard the word; for they heard them speak with tongues." At Ephesus, the grammatical inference is that *all* twelve men who received the Spirit spoke with tongues and prophesied. Therefore, all who receive the Baptism in the Spirit today also speak with tongues.

CHAPTER XII

The Baptism in the Holy Spirit, Available for Us Today

IN this chapter we shall seek to show that the Baptism in the Holy Spirit is available for all Christians. In the words of R. A. Torrey:

Nevertheless, the baptism with the Holy Spirit is the birthright of every believer. It was purchased for us by the atoning death of Christ, and when He ascended to the right hand of the Father, He received the promise of the Father and shed Him forth upon the church, and if anyone today has not the baptism with the Holy Spirit as a personal experience, it is because he has not claimed his birthright.[1]

---

[1] R. A. Torrey, *The Person and Work of the Holy Spirit* (Fleming H. Revell, New York [c. 1910]), p. 177.

Jonathan Goforth also declares:

The Scriptures convey no other meaning to me than that the Lord Jesus planned that the Holy Spirit should continue among us in as mighty manifestation as at Pentecost. The efficacy of the Baptism of the Holy Ghost and of fire dies down in any soul only when that soul willfully quenches it.[1]

IF OLD TESTAMENT SAINTS, WHY NOT WE?

We have already noted the scriptures which tell us concerning Joseph, Moses, Bezaleel, Joshua, the seventy elders, Othniel, Gideon, Jephthah, Saul, David, Nathan, Gad, Samson, Amasai, Azariah, Ezekiel, Daniel, Joel, Hosea, Amos, Obadiah, Jonah, Micah, Nahum, Habakkuk, Haggai, Zephaniah, Zechariah the Second, Malachi, John the Baptist, Zacharias, Elisabeth, and Simeon, who were all filled with the Holy Spirit.

Of most of them it is recorded that they spoke out in prophecy under the inspiration of the Holy Spirit. These lived under the law, a different dispensation from the Christians of apostolic days, and the first named lived about sixteen hundred years previous to the day of Pentecost. Is it reasonable to think that we, who live in New Testament days, under

---

[1]Jonathan Goforth, *By My Spirit*, p 12, as quoted by Elmer C. Miller, *Pentecost Examined* (Gospel Publishing House, Springfield, Mo., 1936), p. 43.

the same dispensation of grace in which the Apostles lived, when the Holy Spirit was so generously outpoured and hardly further away in point of time than certain ones in Old Testament times who received this blessing, should not be allowed to receive the same Holy Spirit in the same wonderful way as they? God is no respecter of persons. Romans 2:11. Why should we be denied this blessing and privilege just because we, by the accident of birth, find ourselves living nineteen hundred years after the Day of Pentecost?

PREDICTIONS OF GENERAL OUTPOURING INCLUDED ALL

The prediction concerning the general outpouring of the Spirit given by Isaiah, Jeremiah, Ezekiel and Joel, as already cited, all set no restriction or limitation upon that outpouring. Upon all flesh: sons, daughters, old men, young men, servants, handmaidens, Jews, and Gentiles. Why should we, and how can we, exempt ourselves from this universal blessing?

OUTPOURING TO COME IN THESE LATTER DAYS

Joel specifically declared that this general diffusion of the Holy Spirit was to come in the latter days (or last days, the meaning of the Hebrew word "acherith," as shown by the more accurate translation of the passage when quoted by Peter on the day of Pentecost). To confirm the time identification of the outpouring, Joel goes on to say, "And I will shew wonders in the heavens and in the earth, blood, and fire, and pillars of smoke. The sun shall be turned into darkness, and the moon into blood, before the great and the terrible day of the Lord come." Joel 2:30-31. This is a reference to the great tribulation spoken of by the Lord Himself and described fully in the book of Revelation. The tribulation is to come at the end of the church age. We are now living in the end of the church age. Therefore this is especially the time when the outpouring of the Spirit prophesied by Joel is to come to pass. It is coming to pass, on schedule. It is here, available for us today.

The latter rain that shall precede the coming spiritual harvest will probably be another Pentecost-like effusion of the Holy Ghost.[1]

A QUOTATION FROM ROBERT C. McQUIL-KIN

Peter said that the outpouring of the Spirit at Pentecost was in fulfillment of that prophecy of Joel: "And it shall be in the last days, saith God, I will pour of My Spirit upon all flesh." Now it is evident that this prophecy was not completely fulfilled at Pentecost, nor has it been fulfilled in any day since. There still remain these wonders in heav-

---

[1] Jamieson, Faussett, and Brown (Geo. H. Doran Co., New York), p. 493.

en above and on the earth beneath that shall precede the great and terrible "day of the Lord"; we
still await that day when the sun shall be turned
into darkness and the moon into blood. Acts 2:17-
21. But if the prophecy still awaits a further and
more complete fulfillment, shall we say that the
Spirit of God may not again be poured out in
mighty power and in supernatural demonstrations?
There seems to be trustworthy evidence that these
supernatural manifestations have occurred from
time to time through the ages, in individual cases.
There is nothing in Scripture to make such working of God impossible; rather we might expect
that they should occur. And is it not reasonable to
expect that in connection with the culminating
judgments of this age and the ushering in of
a new age there should be a mighty outpouring of
the Spirit of God? It is this expectation of a special
"latter rain" outpouring that has led many earnest
Christians into the Pentecostal movement.[2]

THE BAPTISM IN THE SPIRIT FOR THE WHOLE CHURCH AGE

The Baptism in the Holy Spirit is particularly
identified with the church age, for it became general
at the ushering in of this age. It is God's method
whereby the Holy Spirit may possess men completely
and be able to control them and operate through

---

[2]Robt. C. McQuilkin, *What Is Pentecost's Message Today?*
(Sunday School Times, Philadelphia), p. 27.

them in the accomplishment of His own purpose. Has the Church age ended? Has the Holy Spirit been taken out of this world? Has God's plan changed? If so, where and how has He indicated the change? There is no Scriptural intimation of a change in God's plan during the church age or before He comes to take His bride home. Why should we merely assume there has been a change in God's plan? Why not rather believe that His promises are yea and amen, and available for us today as well as for those who lived closer to the time when they were uttered?

TESTIMONY OF A. J. GORDON AND A. MAHAN

We must withhold our consent from the inconsistent exegesis which would make the water baptism of the apostolic times still rigidly binding, but would relegate the Baptism in the Spirit to a bygone dispensation. We hold indeed, that Pentecost was once for all, but equally that the appropriation of the Spirit by believers is always for all, and that the shutting up of certain great blessings of the Holy Ghost within that ideal realm called "the apostolic age," however convenient it may be as an escape from fancied difficulties, may be the means of robbing believers of some of their most precious covenant rights.[1]

---

[1]A. J. Gordon, *The Ministry of the Spirit* (Fleming H. Revell, New York [c. 1894]), p. 72.

The promise of the Spirit does not pertain merely to the Apostles, the primitive church, or a favored few in subsequent ages. It is, on the other hand, the common gift to all who believe in Christ, the least as well as the greatest, to the end of time. . . . Neither is there any gift He is more willing to bestow upon believers than this Divine Baptism. . . . This Baptism is the noblest blessing of Christianity, and no other can fill its place.[1]

SIGN VALUE OF THE GIFTS

Concerning the gifts of the Spirit, it is true that there is an element of a sign value in them. The miracles which Moses and Aaron wrought in Egypt were a sign to Pharaoh, as well as a punishment to him and his people. The miracles which Moses worked before the Children of Israel as they traveled through the wilderness on their way to Canaan were proof that Moses was God's man, as well as a means of providing them with food and deliverance. The miracles of Christ also were to be His credentials before a doubting multitude, as well as to express His power and His love and to give deliverance to hundreds of sufferers. "Believe me for the very work's sake." John 14:11. These "signs" shall follow them that believe. Mark 16:17. And they

---

[1]A. Mahan, *Baptism of the Holy Ghost,* pp. 48 49, as quoted in J. Elder Cumming, *Through the Eternal Spirit.* Ibid., p. 78.

that heard Him went out preaching, "God also bearing them witness, both with signs and wonders, and with divers miracles, and gifts of the Holy Ghost, according to His own will." Hebrews 2:4.

SIGNS ARE NEEDED TODAY

Have we no unbelieving Egyptians today? Are there no gainsaying Israelites today? Is there no need today for credentials for the workers of God? Is there no need for the power of God to be manifested today? There are sick today in need of healing. There have been physicians since Joseph was embalmed in Egypt, but this does not preclude the need of the working of the power of God. The very fact that the gifts of the Spirit are for signs is proof that they are needed today and therefore available for us today. If the devil will be smart enough to use signs and wonders to deceive in the last days (2 Thess. 2:9; Rev. 13:13, 14; Rev. 16:14) will God be any less wise and powerful?

Let us not limit God in His working, and let us not fail to be ready for new and great outpourings of the Holy Spirit in the closing days of this age. For the days are upon us when nothing will avail to break through the overwhelming power of the enemy except supernatural power beyond what most Christians have known anything about.[1]

---

[1] Robt. C. McQuilkin, op. cit., p. 27.

GIFTS ARE FOR ALL WHO BELIEVE

When Jesus spoke of the coming of the Spirit and the accompanying gifts of power, He did not limit them to His immediate successors. *"He that believeth on me, as the Scripture hath said, out of his belly shall flow rivers of living water. But this spake He of the Spirit which they that believe on Him should receive."* John 7:38,39. The receiving of the Spirit and the flowing of rivers of living water are promised by the Lord to THEM THAT BELIEVE. "Verily, verily, I say unto you, *He that believeth on me, the works that I do shall he do also, and greater works than these shall he do because I go unto my father."* John 14:12. Again, those works are said to be done by HIM THAT BELIEVETH. "And these signs shall follow *them that believe;* In my name they shall cast out devils; they shall speak with new tongues; they shall take up serpents; and if they drink any deadly thing, it shall not hurt them; they shall lay hands on the sick and they shall recover." Mark 16:17-18. Whom shall these signs follow? THEM THAT BELIEVE. If these promises of Christ are not fulfilled in the lives of men today, it is evident that the simple and only reason is, THEY DO NOT BELIEVE.

TONGUES SHALL CEASE WHEN JESUS COMES

A verse in 1 Corinthians 13 is taken by some to mean that the gift of the Spirit has ceased and vanished away. "Charity never faileth: but whether there be prophecies, they shall fail; whether there be tongues, they shall cease: whether there be knowledge, it shall vanish away." v. 8. The context of this verse must be read to understand it. "For we know in part, and we prophesy in part. But when that which is perfect is come, then that which is in part shall be done away. When I was a child, I spake as a child, I understood as a child, I thought as a child: but when I became a man, I put away childish things. For now we see through a glass, darkly: but then face to face; now I know in part; but then shall I know even as also I am known." vv. 9-12. In these verses, 8 to 12, we have a comparison of love with the gifts of prophecy, tongues, and the words of knowledge. Love is declared to be the greatest, since it will endure when the others shall have finished their purpose and shall have passed away. It is stated that the time will come when these gifts of the Spirit will cease to operate. When is that time? When will that which is perfect come? When shall we see face to face? When shall I know even as also I am known? It is apparent that all four of these questions have the same answer. The answer is, When Jesus comes. Then shall we all see face to face in heaven, there where knowledge shall be complete. Then and then only shall the gifts cease. Since Jesus and heaven have not yet come, this scripture proves that these gifts, and their parent, the Baptism in the Spirit, are available for us today.

[99]

The bounds set to the exercise of these gifts is "when that which is perfect is come," which scholarship has generally held to mean, when the Lord Himself shall return to earth. The gift of tongues and of prophecy therefore do not seem to be confined within the first age of the church.[1]

---

[1] A. J. Gordon, op., cit., p. 55.

CHAPTER XIII

The Baptism in the Holy Spirit, How to Receive It

LET US NOW RECEIVE

AFTER having seen that the Baptism in the Holy Spirit is an experience distinct from conversion, that it is a most desirable blessing, and that it is available for us today, we are ready to ask, "How may we receive this experience?" To give intellectual assent to a conclusion and to accept a doctrine as theologically sound are good as far as they go. But these will be of little value to us personally unless we take definite hold of the promises of God and enter experientially into that realm and blessing in which we have come to believe. For those who are ready to enter into this blessed experience, we offer some words of suggestion.

WE MUST FIRST BE SAVED

The first matter that must be settled as we approach God to receive the Baptism in the Spirit, is that of being right with God. It is impossible for a sinner to receive the Baptism in the Spirit. "He shall give you another Comforter . . . *whom the world cannot receive.*" John 14:16, 17. The world cannot receive Him. This is an impossibility. God cannot deny Himself. He cannot bless evil. He cannot come into an unclean vessel which has not yielded itself to Him. There must be a definite born-again experience as preparation for receiving the Baptism in the Spirit. The blood is first applied, and then the oil. We must first pray through to a know-so salvation in which the Spirit witnesses with our spirits that we are children of God. Romans 8:16.

WE MUST OBEY

"And we are his witnesses of these things: and so is also the Holy Ghost, whom God hath given to them that obey Him." Acts 5:32. Here arises the question of a possible controversy with God. If there is any measure of rebellion against Him, that issue will have to be settled with a perfect surrender to Him. It is only as we walk in the light that we have fellowship with God and the blood of Jesus Christ His Son cleanseth us from all sin. 1 John 1:7.

Rejectors Are Not Obedient.

Here we might ask, How can His children walk

in the light and be obedient, when they have not received the Holy Spirit? He told His disciples to go and make other disciples and teach them to observe all things that He had commanded them. Matt. 28: 20. He had commanded them not to depart from Jerusalem until they had been filled with power from on high. Luke 24:49. This command was to be passed on to their converts, the new disciples. His command then comes also to us. It is stated in Ephesians 5:18: "Be filled with the Spirit." Can we be obedient children and disobey that command? If the five hundred brethren by whom He was seen after His resurrection (1 Cor. 15:6) heard His command to tarry in the city of Jerusalem, and only 120 obeyed and received the Spirit, then 380 of them did not obey, and, not obeying, did not receive. They did not tarry as He commanded. Hence, they did not qualify to receive. No wonder that thousands do not receive the Baptism in the Spirit today. They do not obey the command to tarry until they receive.

WE MUST ASK

"If ye then, being evil, know how to give good gifts unto your children; how much more shall your heavenly Father give the Holy Spirit to *them that ask him?*" Luke 11:13. Here is the kindness, the generosity, the willingness, and the impartiality of our wonderful heavenly Father. He is able to give the Holy Spirit to all that *ask* Him. He is willing to give the Holy Spirit to all that ask Him. He is more willing and anxious to give than we, as parents, are to give to our children. The only restraint that can be placed upon Him is that which our lack of desire imposes. He gives the Holy Spirit only to them that *ask* Him. "Ye have not because ye *ask* not." James 4:2. This is God's elimination test to determine whom He considers worthy to receive this priceless gift. It is without money and without price, but He will give it only to those who *ask* for it. "Let us therefore come boldly unto the throne of Grace." Heb. 4:16. We must not ask with leaden lips. We should offer Him "the fruit of our lips." Heb. 13:15.

We Must Ask Importunately.

Shall we ask once and let that suffice? Shall we consider that He gave the Spirit to us when asked once, even though there be no evidence then or thereafter that He came? Or shall we shrug our shoulders and say, "It's not our fault. We asked and nothing happened. What more can we do?" No, let us rather read: "Ask, and it shall be given you; seek, and ye shall find; knock, and it shall be opened unto you." Matthew 7:7. Does not this scripture imply degrees in asking? If asking once does not yield immediate results, then seek. This pictures to us the woman who lost the coin and sought diligently until she found it. And if this process does not yield results as quickly as we would like, then knock. This is insistence and persistence. Who was it that gave us the two parables to illustrate importunity in prayer: the importunate widow who came to the unjust judge, and the friend who came to his friend at midnight asking for bread? "I say unto you, though he will not rise and give him, because he is his friend, yet because of his importunity, he will rise and give him as many as he needeth. And I say unto you, Ask, and it shall be given you; seek, and ye shall find; knock, and it shall be opened unto you." Luke 11:8, 9. This very passage concludes with the promise to give the Holy Spirit to them that ask him. v. 13. This constitutes Christ's instruction to keep on asking until we receive the Holy Spirit.

WE MUST BELIEVE

"That we might receive the promise of the Spirit *through faith*." Gal. 3:14. "The Holy Spirit which they that *believe* on Him should receive." John 7:39. "He that cometh to God must believe that he is, and that he is a rewarder of them that diligently seek him." Heb. 11:6. Askers, seekers, knockers after the Baptism in the Spirit, should always remember that this experience is also called, "The Gift of the Holy Ghost." Gifts are not earned or won by price or merit. Gifts cannot be forced from the giver. Leaping upon the altar or cutting ourselves with lancets will not force our God any more than Baal was forced. 1 Kings 18:26-28. It isn't loud shouting that will bring Him nor repetitions of phrases of praise; although loud shouting and much praising of God are Scriptural, and therefore in order, if we are so impelled. Psalm 98:4; Psalm 150;

Psalm 67:3,5; Luke 19:37-40. But we cannot pay for the gift even in this way. The Holy Spirit is a gracious, glorious, God-sent Gift, and we receive Him by faith and by faith alone. There is a "rest of faith" into which we must enter. "For he that is entered into his rest, he also hath ceased from his own works, as God did from his." Heb. 4:10.

Elements of Faith.

Faith in God consists of utter lack of dependence on ourselves or on others and a knowledge that only God has what we need and want. We must believe that He will give only as a gift, but that He will give freely as we meet His conditions and ask Him for His gifts. So we first make sure that we are right with God. Then we cease from our own works or efforts, and apply to Him for the gift which we seek. He is waiting for us to come to this point. "And therefore will the Lord wait, that he may be gracious unto you." Isa. 30:18. We then wait together: He, to see if we are earnest, sincere and hungry; we, to prove that we are. "Blessed are all they that wait for him." Isa. 30:18c. "But they that wait upon the Lord shall renew their strength." Isa. 40:31. "Wait on the Lord: be of good courage, and he shall strengthen thine heart: wait, I say, on the Lord." Psa. 27:14. "Blessed is the man that heareth me, watching daily at my gates, waiting at the posts of my doors." Prov. 8:34. While it is true that the disciples tarried for that first Pentecostal blessing because the day of Pentecost had not yet fully come, it is also true that waiting or tarrying before the Lord is always Scriptural and is normal procedure in receiving from God.

Faith Rejoices.

Faith is more than waiting on God. Faith expects. A seeker for the Baptism in the Spirit waits before God continually, and definitely expects while he waits. A child awaits punishment with a sad countenance and drooping spirits; he awaits his share of the delicacy or his Christmas present with great joy and delight. One awaits the receipt of the Baptism in the Spirit with joy and delight. That joy and delight will be the register of his appreciation of the gift or of his real expectancy of it. If he is not happy as he waits, he either does not consider the gift worth being happy about, or else he really does not expect to receive it. This joy and delight will be expressed toward God, for He is the Giver of the expected Gift. "Let all those that seek thee rejoice and be glad in thee." Psa. 40:16.

Faith Receives.

Joy and delight toward God are expressed by words of praise. "Thank you, Lord Jesus"; "I praise thee, Lord"; "Glory"; "Hallelujah"; "Praise God," etc. This "sacrifice of praise to God continually, that is, the fruit of our lips giving thanks to His name" (Heb. 13:15), is a sacrifice in that it is offered upon His altar, not that it is a sacrifice to give it. In this state of joyous expectancy, we reach out to receive from our God the blessing He has promised. Faith is the hand that reaches out and receives the gift of the Holy Spirit. "Him that cometh to me, I will in no wise cast out." John 6:37. Never yet has a child of God approached his Father along this pathway and been disappointed. "Faithful is he that calleth you, who also will do it." 1 Thess. 5:24.

APOSTLES PRAYED AND PRAISED

It remains now to look into the Scriptural precedents in this matter of receiving the Baptism in the Holy Spirit. If being a Christian first, obeying, asking, and believing are the steps into this experience, then these are the steps which were taken by the early disciples as well as by all others. The twelve, or rather the eleven, were told to tarry in the city of Jerusalem until they be endued with power from on high. Luke 24:49. "These all continued with one accord in prayer and supplication." Acts 1:14. "And were continually in the temple, praising and blessing God." Luke 24:53. They obeyed and waited; they asked by prayer and supplication (insistent asking); they believed and expressed their faith by praising and blessing God. Did He meet them on this pathway of faith? "They were all filled with the Holy Ghost, and began to speak with other tongues as the Spirit gave them utterance." Acts 2:4.

SAMARITANS BELIEVED AND WERE PRAYED FOR

At Samaria, Philip's converts believed the things concerning the kingdom of God and the name of Jesus Christ, and were baptized both men and women. Acts 8:12. Peter and John came down from Jerusalem to tell them about the baptism in the Holy Spirit, for as yet He was fallen on none of them. No revival ought to be allowed to go on long without the Baptism in the Spirit being received. So thought the apostles which were at Jerusalem, and so is the eternal truth. Peter and John prayed for them, that they might receive the Holy Ghost. Acts 8:15. Peter had told the Sanhedrin that the Holy Ghost was given to them that obey God (Acts 5:32), and so he doubtless explained this to the Samaritan converts. Peter and John both had heard the Lord promise that the Father would give the Holy Spirit to them that ask Him. So they surely told this, too, to the Samaritan converts. When these awaiting new disciples were thus prayed for and instructed, the apostles laid hands on them (as an aid to the seeker's faith) and they received the Holy Ghost. Acts 8:17. "Believe in the Lord your God, so shall ye be established; believe his prophets, so shall ye prosper." 2 Chron. 20:20. God honored His servants by imparting the Holy Spirit through the laying on of their hands that the people might honor them as God-appointed and God-accompanied leaders.

PAUL PRAYED AND WAS PRAYED FOR

Paul was converted on the way to Damascus and, being blinded, was led by the hand into the city. He had called Jesus Lord, and none can do this except by the Holy Ghost. 1 Cor. 12:3. After three days, the Lord told Ananias—a devout disciple— to go and inquire for one called Saul, of Tarsus; "for behold, he prayeth." Acts 9:11. He was a Christian (Ananias called him brother); he had obeyed Christ by coming into Damascus to hear the things which the Lord there had to tell him; he was now praying or asking things of God. He may not have known what he needed, but God knew, and sent Ananias that he might receive his sight and be filled with the Holy Ghost. Ananias put his hands on him as he prayed for him. This is a method which is common in Divine practice. Jesus touched Peter's wife's mother, and she arose and ministered unto them. Matthew 8:15. On His second trip to Nazareth, He laid hands on a few sick folk and healed them. Mark 6:5. He had promised that these signs should follow them that believe: "they shall lay hands on the sick, and they shall recover." Mark 16:18. Paul and Barnabas were sent out as the church's first missionaries after the church leaders had laid their hands upon them. Acts 13:3. This is a symbol that the one who is praying is a channel through whom the power of the Lord is conveyed— for healing or for blessing.

CORNELIUS' HOUSEHOLD R E C E I V E D SUDDENLY

At Cornelius' household, the sovereignty of God intervened in a special way. "While Peter was yet speaking, the Holy Ghost fell on them." Acts 10:44. This is always God's privilege. How foolish and futile is the attempt to put God into a strait jacket or to arrange His ways of working in set sequence. Peter had told the Pentecostal audience, "Repent, and be baptized, . . . and ye shall receive the gift of the Holy Ghost." Acts 2:38, 39. But at Cornelius' home, his converts believed, received the Holy Ghost, and then were baptized. Acts 10:44-48. Why not? Just so it is all done in obedience to God, and to the best of one's ability, and according to the light one has. Who wouldn't welcome other sovereign interventions in the pouring out of the Holy Ghost as it happened at Cornelius' household? Could we not even consider that this visitation was God's ideal, His perfect pattern: believe Christ, receive the Holy Spirit in immediate succession?

EPHESIANS BELIEVED AND WERE PRAYED FOR

At Ephesus, Paul carefully instructed those disciples of John, laid hands on them and they, too, received the Holy Spirit. Who would say that he did not instruct them according to the pattern which had been followed theretofore? It is the once-for-all pattern: be saved, obey God, ask Him for His blessings, believe with all your heart, and ye shall receive the fullness of the Holy Spirit.

He gave Him to His church, to be its permanent possession during the present age; and He waits to give each individual member of that church his or her share in Pentecost, on the one condition of applying for it by faith. As you took forgiveness from the hand of the dying Christ, take your share of the Pentecostal gift from the hand of the living Christ.[1]

---

[1]F. B. Meyer, *Back to Bethel*, p. 94, as quoted in Elmer C. Miller, *Pentecost Examined* (Gospel Publishing House, Springfield, Mo., 1936), p. 29.

CHAPTER XIV

The Gifts of the Spirit

WE SHOULD STUDY SPIRITUAL GIFTS

NOW concerning spiritual gifts, brethren, I would not have you ignorant." 1 Cor. 12:1. The description of the spiritual gifts which follows is of a definite phase of the work and ministry of the Holy Spirit. Among these gifts are those of tongues and interpretation, which are particularly noticable in the Pentecostal Movement. It belongs therefore to a treatise on Pentecostal truth that a thorough study be made of the whole realm of spiritual gifts.

GIFTS CLASSIFIED

The gifts of the Spirit, as listed in First Cor. 12, can be classified in three groups. There are three gifts of revelation, three gifts of power, and three gifts of utterance. The gifts of the word of wisdom, the word of knowledge, and discerning of spirits are grouped as gifts of revelation. Faith, miracles, and healings are the gifts of power. And the gifts of utterance are prophecy, tongues, and interpretation.

WISDOM GREATEST IN ITS CLASS

The order of the gifts in these groups can easily be ascertained. Inasmuch as wisdom presupposes knowledge and is an advance on knowledge itself, being the ability to use knowledge discreetly, it is clear that wisdom is greater than knowledge. Discerning of spirits, or knowing spirits, is but one section of the vast realm of knowledge and is therefore less than the gift of the word of knowledge. The order then of this group is: *wisdom, knowledge,* and *discerning of spirits.*

FAITH GREATEST IN ITS CLASS

The gifts of healings refer to the divine power to effect deliverance from sickness and disease. The gift of miracles naturally would be still greater than the gifts of healing because of the near creative element which exists in them. Miracles are more pronounced and spectacular than healings. Then we come to the great power of faith itself. This is the power by which the worlds were made. God spoke and it came to pass. Joshua commanded the sun and the moon to stand still, and they obeyed him. Jesus said: "If ye have faith as a grain of mustard seed, ye shall say unto this mountain, Remove hence to yonder place; and it shall remove; and nothing shall be impossible unto you." Matt. 17:20. It is evident then that faith is the greatest of the gifts of power. Their order is: *faith, miracles,* and *healings.*

[114]

PROPHECY GREATEST IN ITS CLASS

1 Cor. 14:5 declares that greater is he that prophesieth than he that speaketh with tongues, except he interpret. Thus tongues plus interpretation equal prophecy, and prophecy is the greatest of these gifts of utterance. Interpretation depends upon tongues and therefore is less than tongues. The order here, then, is: *prophecy, tongues,* and *interpretation.*

PROPHECY GREATEST OF ALL

Paul said, "Covet earnestly the best gifts." 1 Cor. 12:31. He meant therefore the gifts of wisdom, faith, and prophecy; for they are the greatest in their respective groups. Likewise Paul enjoined the Corinthians to desire spiritual gifts, but rather that they might prophesy. 1 Cor. 14:1, 39. The reason for this emphasis on prophecy must be because it is the gift which serves not only its own purpose of giving God's message in the power of the Holy Spirit, but is a channel through which the gifts of faith, knowledge and wisdom find expression and utterance. As the Holy Spirit is the agent of God and of Christ, and also operates in His own right, so prophecy is an agent for other gifts and is also a gift itself.

TEACHING AND EXHORTATION

Turning to the 12th of Romans, we find another list of gifts which fits in as supplementary to the official list as given in First Corinthians 12. The first of those mentioned in Rom. 12:6 is the gift of prophecy, which is in the list of First Corinthians 12, and finds particular emphasis in 1 Cor. 14:39. This is a tie-in with the other list of gifts and confirms that the gifts mentioned in Romans 12 are likewise gifts of the Spirit. The other gifts listed here are teaching, exhortation, ministering, giving, ruling, and showing mercy. The first two of these seem to be a blending of the gifts of prophecy and wisdom and knowledge. When one gives forth the word of knowledge under the power of the Holy Spirit in a way that imparts the knowledge to others, he is operating in the gift of teaching. When the evangelist uses great wisdom in his preaching under the anointing of the Spirit he is exercising the gift of exhortation. Of Stephen it was said, "And they were not able to resist the wisdom and the Spirit by which he spake." Acts 6:10.

MINISTERING, RULING, GIVING, SHOWING MERCY

The ministry referred to in Rom. 12:7 is that of serving in the church. When Paul and Barnabas started on their first missionary journey they had John Mark "to their minister." Acts 13:5. This means that he was their attendant or one who ministered to their material needs. The word for deacon, as found in 1 Tim. 3:8, comes from the same root-stem which is translated "minister" in Rom. 12:7. Thus the deacon who serves in material matters of the church is a minister and should have the gift of ministering, which is a gift of the Spirit.

This gift is doubtless properly classified as a gift of wisdom and power. In this group also are ruling, giving, and showing mercy. It must be noted that this type of service is exalted and holy in the sight of God. There is an enduement with power from on high to enable one to serve in these capacities. These gifts operate according to the grace that is given to us and hence are gifts of grace from our God.

OTHER REFERENCES TO GIFTS

Other references to gifts of the Spirit which are to be found in the New Testament are in 1 Peter 4:10-11; 1 Cor. 1:5,7; 2 Cor. 8:7; and 1 Thess. 5:19-21. Peter mentions the gifts of utterance and says "if any man speak, let him speak as the oracles of God." He, too, mentions the gift of ministry and exhorts, "let him do it as of the ability which God giveth." In the first chapter of 1 Corinthians Paul refers to their having been enriched in all utterance and in all knowledge, and declares that they came behind in no gift. He refers to the gifts of utterance: prophecy, tongues, and interpretation; and the gifts of wisdom, knowledge and discerning of spirits. But he makes the plain statement that all of the gifts are to be found in the Corinthian church. In his second letter, he specifically included the gifts of faith (faith, miracles, and healings) as well as those of utterance and knowledge. In 1 Thess. 5:19-21, Paul is exhorting the church at Thessalonica to allow the gifts of the Spirit full operation among them and by no mean to despise them, particularly prophesyings.

The Pulpit Commentary adds this note on "Quench not the Spirit," 1 Thess. 5:19: "By the Spirit here is usually understood the miraculous gifts of the Spirit—speaking with tongues or prophesyings; and it is supposed that the apostle here forbids the exercise of these gifts being hindered or checked."[1]

GIFTS OF THE SPIRIT DISTINGUISHED FROM THE GIFT OF THE SPIRIT

The gifts of the Spirit must be distinguished from the gift of the Spirit. "Ye shall receive the gift of the Holy Ghost," Peter said to his audience on the day of Pentecost. This is the Baptism or the filling with the Holy Spirit which the 120 had just received, evidenced by the speaking with other tongues as the Spirit gave utterance. The gifts of the Spirit are given by the Holy Spirit as a part of His ministry and control over the believer who has let Him come upon him in His fullness. The Holy Spirit, as the Spirit of Christ, does come into the heart of the born-again child of God, and ministers to him in regenerative capacity. It is only at and after His coming upon one in baptismal fullness, that He takes definite control as the Holy Spirit is His own right and in His own ministry. He then begins to dispense His gifts severally as He wills. Gifts are manifestations of the Spirit, the shining forth of Him who is within.

---

[1] *Pulpit Commentary*, Vol. 48, p. 105.

ALL BELIEVERS RECEIVE HIS NATURE.

This is not to say that children of God in whom dwells the Spirit of Christ and who have not received the Baptism in the Spirit will not have varying measures of wisdom, knowledge, faith, etc. which come from the Lord. Being partakers of His nature and dwelling in Christ as the branch in the vine, naturally bring one a measure of the qualities which Christ has. But as Christ Himself received a mighty Baptism in the Spirit which marked a great change in His ministry, anointing Him with the Holy Spirit and with power, so the Baptism in the Spirit today brings a person into a place of anointing and power where the full complement of the gifts of the Spirit may be manifest and operative in his life.

GIFTS NOT AN EVIDENCE OF HOLINESS

All who possess the gifts of the Spirit do not necessarily have superior holiness. James reminds us that "Elias was a man subject to like passions as we are." James 5:17. Elijah's flight from Jezebel and his despair of life under the juniper tree evidence that fact. And yet he had exercised the greatest of the gifts of power, namely the gift of faith, in a way which has never since been excelled. When Peter and John used this gift in the healing of the lame man at the Gate Beautiful, Peter explained carefully, "Ye men of Israel, why marvel ye at this? or why look ye so earnestly on us, as though by our own power or holiness we had made this man to walk?" Acts 3:12.

The power of the gift of faith (the faith which is by Him, v. 16) operates apart from human power or holiness. Paul said frankly, "Though I speak with the tongues of men and of angels, and have not charity, I am become as sounding brass, or a tinkling cymbal. And though I have the gift of prophecy, and understanding all mysteries, and all knowledge; and though I have all faith, so that I could remove mountains, and have not charity, I am nothing." 1 Cor. 13:1, 2. This means that it is possible to have the gifts—the best gifts and many gifts—and not to have love with them, which reduces them to no value. The Corinthian church came behind in no gift, and yet they were carnal. 1 Cor. 3:1-3. A final instance is that of Samson. He was not godly on all occasions, yet mighty miracles were wrought by him.

GIFTS NOT TO BE DESPISED

Let no one disdain gifts on this account. What God creates and gives is good to have. It is a part of His divine plan for the furtherance of His gospel and program. We should accept all of His provision, gifts, and graces, and keep all in the right proportion and balance.

CHAPTER XV

The Word of Knowledge

KNOWLEDGE BEFORE WISDOM AND
    TEACHING

WE come now to a detailed examination of the group of gifts which have to do with knowing: the word of wisdom, the word of knowledge, and discerning of spirits. These gifts operate in the mental realm. In considering the distinction between wisdom and knowledge, let us note first the simple definition, "wisdom is knowledge rightly applied." Knowledge is a prerequisite to wisdom and to teaching. Teaching is imparting knowledge. No teacher can teach without first knowing. But not all who know are able to teach. Teaching is causing another to learn. It is the art of imparting knowledge, skill in transferring knowledge to others. Teaching is, therefore, a kind of wisdom itself. Wisdom proper is discreet action on the basis of knowledge.

AN ILLUSTRATION OF THIS

For example, knowing how to walk, knowing a shelter is near by, knowing that I will get wet if I do not move into the shelter before it rains, I therefore am wise enough to move where I will be sheltered. Action on the basis of knowledge is wisdom. Upon the basis of His infinite knowledge of the effects which follow certain causes and of ways and means of producing certain ends, God wisely brings into existence certain beings, sets in motion certain influences and allows certain things to continue, while restraining others. The grand result at the end of time will be that He is glorified by having displayed Himself—His grace, His power, His wrath, and His infinite love. "Oh, the depths of the riches both of the wisdom and knowledge of God! how unsearchable are His judgments, and His ways past finding out." Rom. 11:33.

WHY THE "WORD" OF KNOWLEDGE?

There is significance connected with the fact that these gifts are called the word of wisdom and the word of knowledge rather than merely wisdom and knowledge. When Jesus was called "The Word" (Greek : *Logos*) in John 1:1, 14, this was a title which represented Him as the expression of God. "No man hath seen God at any time: the only begotten Son, who is in the bosom of the Father, He hath declared (revealed) Him." John 1:18. As a word is the audible expression of an invisible thought, so Christ is the tangible expression of the invisible God. In the phrases, the word of wisdom and the word of knowledge, the same word *Logos* is used. These gifts then are expressions of wisdom and knowledge. Not necessarily flashes of fragmentary bits, but degrees of wisdom and knowledge that He, the Sovereign Spirit, wishes to impart. Neither is there a transfer of great reservoirs of wisdom and knowledge, but a "word"—a revelation, an expression—sufficient for the occasion—of the wisdom and knowledge of God.

GOD'S KNOWLEDGE

The gift of the word of knowledge is of and from the Holy Spirit. Since the Holy Spirit is God and knows all things, the knowledge which He gives in this gift is a measure of understanding of the great facts of life and of the universe as they are known to God. This is a mighty reservoir. At His pleasure He dips from this boundless ocean and pours into the understanding of His waiting servants that extent of information and revelation which it pleases Him to give. Peter was right when he told Jesus, "Thou knowest all things." John 21:17. "In Him are hid all the treasures of wisdom and knowledge." Col. 2:3. "Neither is there any creature that is not manifest in His sight; but all things are naked and opened unto the eyes of him with whom we have to do." Heb. 4:13. "Known unto God are all His works from the beginning of the world." Acts 15:18. "Elect according to the foreknowledge of God." 1 Peter 1:2. "For whom He did foreknow, He also did predestinate to be conformed to the image of His Son." Romans 8:29. "Him, being delivered by the determinate counsel and foreknowledge of God." Acts 2:23. "For the eyes of the Lord run to and fro throughout the whole earth." 2 Chron. 16:9.

KNOWLEDGE OF GOD

In addition to the knowledge which God has, there is a knowledge of God which can be dispensed by the Holy Spirit. "The fear of the Lord is the beginning of knowledge." Prov. 1:7. Paul prayed for the Ephesians that God "may give unto you the spirit of wisdom and revelation in the *knowledge of Him*: the eyes of your understanding being enlightened; that ye may *know* what is the hope of his calling, and what the riches of the glory of his inheritance in the saints, and what is the exceeding greatness of his power to usward who believe," etc. Eph. 1:17-19. Again he prayed for them that they "may be able to *comprehend* with all saints what is the breadth, and length, and depth, and height; and to *know* the love of Christ which passeth knowledge (human knowledge)." Eph. 3:18,19. The objective in Christian ministry is that "we all come in the unity of the faith, and of the *knowledge* of the Son of God," etc. Eph. 4:13. For the Colossians he prayed that they might increase in the *knowledge* of God. Col. 1:10. His own personal objective was "that I may *know* Him." Phil. 3:10. But he already had much knowledge of Christ. He said, "when ye read, ye may understand my *knowledge* in the mystery of Christ." Eph. 3:4. "By pureness, by *knowledge*, by long-suffering," etc. 2 Cor. 6:6. "But though I be rude in speech, yet not in *knowledge*." 2 Cor. 11:6. Peter too enjoined, "But grow in grace and in the *knowledge* of our Lord and Savior Jesus Christ." 2 Peter 3:18. Even Moses prayed for himself, "that I may *know* thee." Ex. 33:13. He made *known* His ways unto Moses. Psalm 103:7.

KNOWLEDGE OF HAPPENINGS

It is also true that, in the omnipresence and omniscience of God, He is everywhere present and knows all that is going on everywhere at the same time. Jesus saw Nathanael under the fig tree before He came to him. John 1:48. He knew that Lazarus was dead without being told. John 11:14. He knew the life of the Samaritan woman. John 4:18. Elisha knew the location of the Syrian army and told the king of Israel. 2 Kings 6:8-12. He knew that Gehazi had run after Naaman to ask a present. 2 Kings 5:26. Peter was told that three men from Cornelius were at the gate enquiring for him. Acts 10:19,20. Samuel knew that Saul was coming to him, that his father's asses had been found, and where to find Saul when he hid in the stuff. 1 Samuel 9:15, 16; 10:2; 10:21, 22. These instances and many others like them are examples of bits of knowledge concerning facts and happenings which were supernaturally revealed to the servants of God.

THIS GIFT IMPARTED BY THE SPIRIT

Who can give all this knowledge and information? Can it be acquired by the natural mind?
"For the natural man receiveth not the things of
the Spirit of God, for they are foolishness unto him;
neither can he *know* them, because they are spirit-
ually discerned." 1 Cor. 2:14. "Thou hast hid
these things from the wise and the prudent, and
hast revealed them unto babes." Matt. 11:25.
"Flesh and blood hath not revealed it unto thee,
but my Father which is in heaven." Matt. 16:17.
Revelation of divine truth by the Spirit of truth
is impartation of divine knowledge, a giving of the
Word of Knowledge. A revelation of facts and
happenings is also a part of this gift.

CHAPTER XVI

The Word of Wisdom

GOD'S WISDOM

WISDOM builds with the material which knowledge provides. Wisdom understands all facts, all laws and principles, all trends, influences, possibilities, and inevitabilities. She has all that is needed in the way of subject matter (angelic, human, and natural), power, and skill. Her objective is to bring to pass the great ends which will glorify God, and she sets to work to accomplish those ends. The ability and disposition to use infinite knowledge in the most profitable way, that is the wisdom of God. There is a beautiful personification of wisdom in Prov. 8:22-30: "The Lord possessed me (wisdom) in the beginning of his way, before his works of old. I was set up from the beginning, or ever the earth was. . . . When he prepared the heavens, I was there. . . . Then I was by him, as one brought up with him: and I was daily his delight, rejoicing always before him." "Therefore also said the wisdom of God, I will send them prophets and apostles, and some of them they shall slay and persecute; that the blood of all the prophets which was shed from the foundation of the world, may be required of this generation." Luke 11:49, 50. "For after that in the wisdom of God the world by wisdom knew not God, it pleased God by the foolishness of preaching to save them that believe." 1 Cor. 1:21. His wisdom directed Him in laying out the plan of redemption.

GOD'S ADVICE

"The fear of the Lord is the beginning of wisdom." Prov. 9:10. "The fear of the Lord is to hate evil: pride, arrogancy, and the evil way, and the froward mouth, do I hate." Prov. 8:13. The wisdom of God is written down and expressed in the laws of God. He is advising and instructing the sons of men concerning the path in which they should walk in order to find happiness, peace, and prosperity. "I (wisdom) lead in the way of righteousness, in the midst of the paths of judgment; that I may cause those that love me to inherit substance; and I will fill their treasures." Prov. 8:20, 21. In all of His counsel, His directions, His commandments, and His judgments, He is displaying His wisdom. To heed them will be wisdom on the part of men. "The fear of the Lord—respect, obedience to Him—is the beginning of wisdom." The pronouncements and parables of Christ are the expressions of His and God's wisdom. Yea, Christ is the wisdom of God (1 Cor. 1:24), and "in Him are hid all the treasures of wisdom and knowledge." Col. 2:3. It is wise to do right. God's wisdom tells us what is right.

PERSONAL GUIDANCE

In addition to the general advice which is contained and written in His Word, there are times when God gives specific, personal advice to His children through the word of wisdom. "Then fourteen years after I went up again to Jerusalem with Barnabas, and took Titus with me also. And I went up by revelation and communicated unto them." Gal. 2:1, 2. "Revelation" is a word used for the word of Wisdom. 1 Cor. 14: 6, 26. As the church at Antioch ministered to the Lord and fasted, the Holy Ghost said, "Separate me Barnabas and Saul for the work whereunto I have called them." Acts 13:2. Before the decision to go into Macedonia, Paul had been forbidden of the Holy Ghost to preach the word in Asia, and when they assayed to go into Bithynia the Spirit suffered them not. Acts 16:6, 7. These were times when wisdom was needed in the guidance of the church and its workers. Therefore God spoke to the church at Antioch and to Paul's missionary party through the gift of the word of wisdom.

ANOINTED PREACHING

When the wonderful counsel of God, His provision for man's redemption, and all the appeals of the gospel are presented to men by inspired preachers, the same Spirit of God who moved holy men of old to write the Sacred Scriptures, takes hold of those who proclaim it by word of mouth. "And they were not able to resist the *wisdom* and the spirit by which he spake." Acts 6:10. The word of Wisdom is imparted to those who preach as they present convincing arguments in the power of the Spirit. Paul's proclamation of "Jesus Christ and Him crucified" was presented with the wisdom of God in the power and demonstration of the Holy Ghost. 1 Cor. 2:1-7. And all the more in searching and preaching the deep things of God is the wisdom which comes from heaven needed. 1 Cor. 2:10. This was the ability with which Paul preached, "warning every man and teaching every man in all *wisdom*." Col. 1:28.

CHURCH GOVERNMENT

The "judgments" of the Mosaic law were the interpretations and applications of the Ten Commandments to the practical problems and situations which would arise in the everyday life of the Israelites. So the commandments and counsels of Jesus and of the New Testament which apply to us in our personal lives and church problems need interpretation and application. The Great Administrator of the church is the Holy Spirit. He gives the "word of wisdom" as it is needed in the direction of our lives and in the execution of our Christian tasks and responsibilities. When the murmuring arose among the early disciples concerning the daily administration (Acts 6), the Apostles were given the "word of wisdom" for the occasion. When the church came together to consider the matter of circumcision as necessary for salvation, the wisdom of God was given to James who said, "wherefore my sentence is, that we trouble not them, etc." (Acts 15). In answering the questions and giving instructions concerning the problems of the Corinthians, Paul was given the "word of wisdom." He distinguished between his own mind and the mind of the Lord (1 Cor. 7:6, 10, 25, 40), and with the exceptions which he indicated, he wrote "according to the wisdom given unto him." 2 Peter 3:15. Joseph of old was given wisdom from God as he ministered before Pharaoh. Acts 7:9, 10. Joshua also received wisdom to lead the children of Israel. Deut. 34:9.

PERSONAL REVELATION

Not for the preacher and administrator alone is this wisdom granted. For his converts Paul prayed that God "may give unto you the spirit of *wisdom* and revelation in the knowledge of him," "that ye might be filled with the knowledge of his will in all *wisdom* and spiritual understanding." Eph. 1:17; Col. 1:9. "Who is a wise man and endued with knowledge among you? Let him show out of a good conversation his works with meekness of *wisdom*." James 3:13. This is the wisdom that is from above, and it is available to those who ask in faith. James

3:17; 1:5, 6. "Let the word of Christ dwell in you richly in all *wisdom*." Col. 3:16.

HOLY SPIRIT DEFENSE

There is also the aspect of wisdom in debate or defense. When our Lord was foretelling the persecution which awaited His disciples He promised, "For I will give you a mouth and *wisdom*, which all your adversaries shall not be able to gainsay nor resist." "And when they bring you into the synagogues and unto magistrates, and powers, take ye no thought how or what thing ye shall answer, or what ye shall say: for the Holy Ghost shall teach you in the same hour what ye ought to say." Luke 21:15; 12:11, 12. This is the Holy Spirit's gift of the word of wisdom. This same gift for just such an occasion was manifest perfectly when Christ's adversaries tried to tangle Him in His talk as they asked Him, "Is it lawful to pay tribute to Caesar?" The wisdom of His reply was so complete and His defense so devastating that they marveled at His answer and held their peace. Luke 20:20-26. Stephen's defense before the court of the High Priest was unanswerable and all his enemies could do was to gnash their teeth and stone him. Acts 7.

WISDOM IS PURE

"But the wisdom that is from above is first pure, then peaceable, gentle, and easy to be entreated, full of mercy and good fruits, without partiality and without hypocrisy." James 3:17. This is the only gift of the Spirit which is thus described and to which are ascribed these qualities of good character. This is logical since wisdom is knowing God's will and way toward good behavior. He will not disclose this secret or impart this gift to those who will not walk therein. "Meekness of wisdom" is also referred to by the same writer. James 3:13. This gift is like its Giver, meek and lowly in heart (Matt. 11:29), and imparts its nature to its possessors. By this may men know whether or not the wisdom we have is from above.

CHAPTER XVII

The Discerning of Spirits

IMPORTANT PART OF KNOWLEDGE

THE discerning of spirits is such an important phase of spiritual knowledge that it is honored with recognition apart from the gift of the word of knowledge. The reason for this lies in the value which this gift has in Christian life and ministry.

TWO REALMS OF SPIRITS

The great unseen world of spirits is divided into the good and evil. God and the devil are kings over these respective realms. Cherubim, seraphim, archangels, and angels do the bidding of God. Principalities, powers, rulers of the darkness of this world, wicked spirits in high places, evil spirits, and demons are all under the authority of Satan. These two realms are arrayed against each other, and the war of the ages is still on. God the Holy Spirit is the active Commander in Chief of God's army. He personally indwells and energizes Spirit-filled believers. A valuable weapon both of defense and offense for them is the gift of the discerning of spirits.

SATAN'S STRATEGY

The enemy is not only himself the spirit that now worketh in the children of disobedience; but he has spirits and demons, distinct spirit beings, which he places in the minds and bodies of susceptible unbelievers. His purpose is not only to torment and afflict his victims, but to use them as tools to oppose the gospel and to deceive Christian workers.

DEMON POSSESSION

In the realm of affliction, the Bible speaks of dumb spirits, Matt. 9:32; Mark 9:17; blind spirits, Matt. 12:22; deaf spirits, Mark 9:25; spirits of infirmity, Luke 13:11, 16; and spirits of lunacy, Matt. 17:15, 18. There are also cases of those who were just "possessed with devils (demons)." Matt. 4:24; 8:16, 28; Acts 8:7; 16:16. The gift of discerning of spirits will enable the worker to approach these cases with knowledge and understanding. With the word of authority, he casts out the evil spirit. Mark 16:17.

INSTANCES OF THE OPERATION OF THIS GIFT

When Paul and Barnabas were in the isle of Cyprus, they were resisted in their ministry by Elymas the sorcerer. Paul discerned that he was a child of Satan, and by the word of authority brought God's judgment upon him, smiting him with blindness for a season. Acts 13:6-12. At Philippi a damsel possessed with a spirit of divination "followed Paul and Silas and cried, saying, These men are the servants of the most high God, which show unto us the way of salvation. . . . But Paul, being grieved, turned and said to the spirit, I command thee in the name of Jesus Christ to come out of her. And he came out the same hour." Acts 16:16-18. Here the "gift of discerning of spirits" unmasked this deceiving demon and disclosed him as an enemy in disguise. The spirit had pretended to be a friend and promoter of Paul and his company. Put Paul discerned the true source and motive of this attempted endorsement which was in reality an identification of Paul's message with the spirits of hell. He saw through the devil's trick and rebuked and cast out the evil spirit. This was God's equipment with which Paul was provided and with which God would provide His workers today.

PETER ALSO HAD THIS GIFT

In the case of Ananias the liar, there was not necessarily a lying demon involved, but Peter was able to see through the deceiving action of Ananias and the lying words of Sapphira and expose them publicly. Acts 5:1-11. With Simon the sorcerer, an evil spirit could have lurked behind the pseudo-righteous exterior, although it is not so recorded. But Peter discerned his unregenerate condition, even though it had been hidden from Philip. Acts 8:23. It may be questioned whether discerning of the human spirit is included in the scope of discerning of spirits, but there can be no question about its being a valuable gift.

LAST-DAY DEMONS

Paul's reference to seducing spirits and doctrines of devils (demons) (1 Tim. 4:1) reveals a subtle trick of Satan in conceiving and propagating false doctrines, particularly in the latter times. The gift of "discerning of spirits" could well function here along with the "words of wisdom and knowledge" in exposing and rebuking these spirits of error. In the last days also, the false prophet will perform miracles and signs and lying wonders, in the name of the Antichrist. 2 Thess. 2:9; Rev. 13:14. There will be devils working miracles to call men to Armageddon. Rev. 16:14. There will be no need of the gift of discerning of spirits in the tribulation, or spiritual men left on earth to exercise it. But before the tribulation some lying miracles will without doubt be performed, As Jannes and Jambres withstood Moses, so false miracle workers may counterfeit and oppose the work of God in any age. Discerning of spirits is here also God's answer to these tactics of Satan.

CHAPTER XVIII

The Gifts of Healings

GIFTS OF POWER

THE gifts of power are: faith, workings of miracles, and gifts of healings. These gifts operate in the realm of the physical. They are the gifts of action, which produce signs and wonders. "Grant unto thy servants that . . . signs and wonders may be done by the name of thy holy child Jesus." Acts 4:29, 30. "God also bearing them witness both with signs and wonders, and with divers miracles, and gifts of the Holy Ghost, according to his own will." Heb. 2:4. These gifts of power constituted the "works" with which Jesus' ministry was accompanied and confirmed. "Jesus of Nazareth, a man approved of God among you by miracles and wonders and signs, which God did by him in the midst of you, as ye yourselves also know." Acts 2:22. "Many good works have I shewed you from my Father: for which of those works do ye stone me?" John 10:32. "The Father that dwelleth in me, He doeth the works. Believe me that I am in the Father and the Father in me: or else believe me for the very works' sake. Verily, verily, I say unto you, He that believeth on me, the works that I do shall he do also; and greater works than these shall he do; because I go unto my Father." John 14:10b-12.

HEALINGS MOST FREQUENT OF POWER GIFTS

The "gifts of healings" (both nouns are in the plural in the original) are the most frequently performed of the gifts of power. When Jesus could do no mighty work of power in His own town of Nazareth, He nevertheless was able to lay His hands upon a few sick folk and heal them. Mark 6:5. As when Jesus was on earth, so also today many sick people apply for healing to those who believe. As then, so today, God answers prayer and the sick are healed. Thus it happens that the gifts of healing are the first of the gifts of power that are exercised.

IT IS JESUS' POWER TO HEAL

The gifts of healings, since they are the gifts of the Holy Ghost, are divine enablements to heal the sick apart from the aid of natural means and human skill. "He healed all that were sick; that it might be fulfilled which was spoken by Esaias the prophet, saying, Himself took our infirmities and bare our sicknesses." Matt. 8:16-17. "How God anointed Jesus of Nazareth with the Holy Ghost and with power; who went about doing good, and healing all that were oppressed of the devil; for God was with him." Acts 10:38. "For this reason the Son of God was manifested, that he might destroy the works of the devil." 1 John 3:8. This power of Christ to heal is transferred and conveyed to Spirit-filled believers in and through the "gifts of healings."

SICKNESS IS A RESULT OF THE FALL

"How God anointed Jesus of Nazareth with the Holy Ghost and with power who went about doing good and healing all that were *oppressed of the devil*, for God was with him." Acts 10:38. "And ought not this woman, being a daughter of Abraham, *whom Satan hath bound*, lo, these eighteen years, be loosed from this bond on the sabbath day?" Luke 13:16. This lordship of Satan in the realm of sickness can be traced back to the fall of man in the Garden of Eden. God said, "For in the day that thou eatest thereof thou shalt surely die (dying, thou shalt die)." Gen. 2:17. Adam ate and the death process began. Sickness is the precursor of death. "Death passed upon all men, for that all have sinned." Rom. 5:12. If death reigns over all men, then all men are subject to sickness, its subsidiary. Sickness and death came into the world as a result of man's fall in the garden of Eden and are thus directly involved and included in recovery from the Fall.

HEALING IS IN THE ATONEMENT

Thank God, there is recovery from the Fall and from its disastrous results. "Behold the Lamb of God, which taketh away the sin of the world." John 1:29. "And he is the propitiation for our sins: and not for ours only, but also for the sins of the whole world." 1 John 2:2. He has borne the penalty for our sins and carried the punishment in His body on the cross. "But he was wounded for our transgressions, he was bruised for our iniquities: the chastisement of our peace was upon him: and with his stripes we are healed. . . . The Lord hath laid on him the iniquity of us all." Isa. 53:5, 6. Now, if He took our sins and bore our punishment, should we not expect that He would bear our sicknesses, which are part punishment for our sins? He did just that. In the verse above, quoted from Isaiah, it is stated "with his stripes we are healed." When Matthew quoted from the 53rd chapter of Isaiah, he said, "Himself took our infirmities and bare our sicknesses." Matt. 8:17. Peter said, "Who his own self bare our sins in his own body on the tree, . . . by whose stripes ye were healed." 1 Peter 2:24. James said, "And the prayer of faith shall save the sick, and the Lord shall raise him up; and if he have commited sins, they shall be forgiven him." James 5:15. David wrote, "who forgiveth all thine iniquities; who healeth all thy diseases." Psalm 103:3. Jehovah said, "I am the Lord that healeth thee." Ex. 15: 26. Healing is a part of our redemption right, and that gives us boldness to claim it.

OPERATIONS OF THE GIFTS OF HEALINGS

"And these signs shall follow them that believe: . . . they shall lay hands on the sick, and they shall recover." Mark 16:17, 18. "Is any sick among you? Let him call for the elders of the church, and let them pray over him, anointing him with oil in the name of the Lord, and the prayer of faith shall save the sick, and the Lord shall raise him up." James 5:14, 15. "God hath set in the church . . . gifts of healings." 1 Cor. 12:28. Laying hands on the sick by believers and anointing with oil by the elders are two ways through which the gifts of healings operate. God hath set these gifts in the church. What God hath set, let not man upset!

CHAPTER XIX

The Gift of Faith

FAITH IS THE POWER BY WHICH GOD WORKS

IF ye have faith as a grain of mustard seed, ye shall say unto this mountain, Remove hence to yonder place: and it shall remove; and nothing shall be impossible unto you." Matt. 17:20. "And though I have all faith, so that I could remove mountains, and have not charity, I am nothing." 1 Cor. 13:2. Faith is the power with which God speaks, and by speaking, brings things to pass. "And God said, Let there be light; and there was light." "And God said, Let there be a firmament, . . . and it was so." And so on, for the six days of creation. Gen. 1:3, 6, 7, 9, 14, 20, 24. "Through faith we understand that the worlds were framed by the Word of God, so that things which are seen were not made of things which do appear." Heb. 11:3. This is the power by which Jesus, God's Son, turned the water into wine, multiplied the loaves and fishes, stilled the tempest, cast out devils, and raised the dead. It is the word of divine authority.

WE MAY HAVE GOD'S FAITH

Jesus said, "Have the faith of God." Mark 11:22, R.V. When the gift of faith is operative, it is the faith of God which functions through men. When Peter and John performed the miracle of the healing of the lame man at the Gate Beautiful, Peter explained, "The faith which is by Him hath given him this perfect soundness in the presence of you all." Acts 3:16. When Elijah believed God for the mighty sign of the fire falling upon the water-soaked sacrifice, he prayed, "Let it be known this day . . . that I have done all these things at thy word." 1 Kings 18:36. His instructions were from God and his faith also. When Moses decreed the death of Korah, Dathan, and Abiram and their 250 followers, by the earth's opening her mouth and swallowing them up alive, he said, "Hereby ye shall know that the Lord hath sent me to do all these works; for I have not done them of mine own mind." Numbers 16:28. God had given him instructions what to say and do, and also the faith with which to do it. "And the life which I now live in the flesh I live *by the faith of the Son of God.*" Gal. 2:20.

THE GIFT DEFINED

"If ye abide in me, and my words abide in you, ye shall ask what ye will, and it shall be done unto you." John 15:7. Close contact with God, receiving His instructions, and letting Him exercise His faith through us, constitute having the gift of faith. Elijah said to Ahab, "As the Lord God of Israel liveth, before whom I stand, there shall not be dew nor rain these years, but according to my word." 1 Kings 17:1. This was the gift of faith, bringing things to pass by His word. This verse also gives the secret of the gift—standing before God. Joshua said in the sight of Israel, "Sun, stand thou still upon Gibeon; and thou, Moon, in the valley of Ajalon." Joshua 10:12. Joshua was a man in whom was the Spirit of God. Num. 27:18; Deut. 34;9.

ELIJAH HAD THIS GIFT

Elijah told the widow at Zarephath, "For thus saith the Lord God of Israel, The barrel of meal shall not waste, neither shall the cruse of oil fail, until the day that the Lord sendeth rain upon the earth." 1 Kings 17:14. And it happened according to his word. To the captain of fifty whom Ahaziah sent to take him, Elijah said, "If I be a man of God, then let fire come down from heaven, and consume thee and thy fifty. And there came down fire from heaven and consumed him and his fifty." 2 Kings 1:10.

ELISHA HAD THIS GIFT

Elisha, too, had the gift of faith. He pronounced a curse upon the irreverent children which resulted in their death. 2 Kings 2:23-24. When the kings asked for his help, he said, "Thus saith the Lord, Make this valley full of ditches. For thus saith the Lord, . . . that valley shall be filled with water. . . . And it came to pass . . . that . . . the country was filled with water." 2 Kings 3:16-20. Later he smote the Syrian army with blindness. 2 Kings 6:18.

PAUL HAD THIS GIFT

In the New Testament, in addition to the ministry of Jesus and Peter and John, as already cited, we find Paul smiting Elymas the sorcerer with blindness and casting the demons out of the girl at Philippi. Acts 13:11; 16:18. By the word of authority he healed the lame man at Lystra (Acts 14:10), and by this power he brought Eutychus back to life. Acts 20:12. Faith is the greatest of the gifts of power, and the greatest power in existence.

CHAPTER XX

Workings of Miracles

MIRACLES BY JESUS AND BY THOSE THAT HEARD HIM

STEPHEN was a man full of faith ("grace," R. V.—*charitos*) and of power (*dunameōs*). Acts 6:8. This introduces us to the gift of workings of miracles (both nouns in the plural) as distinct from the gift of faith. Stephen had both gifts. Although they are similar in nature, the Spirit distinguishes between them in 1 Cor. 12:9, 10: "To another faith by the same spirit; . . . to another the working of miracles." "Jesus of Nazareth, a man approved of God among you by miracles (workings of power—*dunamesi*), and wonders and signs, which God did by Him." Acts 2:22. Here is the gift of miracles in Christ's ministry. And the gospel was confirmed by them that heard Him, "God also bearing them witness, both with signs and wonders, and with divers miracles, and gifts of the Holy Ghost, according to His own will." Heb. 2:4. Miracles again, by those that heard Him.

MIRACLES BY PAUL AND PETER

Paul spoke of himself as "he that worketh miracles among you." Gal. 3:5. Signs and wonders and mighty deeds were wrought among them. 2 Cor. 12:12. "And God wrought special miracles by the hands of Paul; so that from his body were brought unto the sick handkerchiefs or aprons, and the diseases departed from them, and the evil spirits went out of them." Acts 19:11, 12. Here was a gift of healing and the power of faith operating through special miracles of power, conveyed by handkerchiefs or aprons. Miracles, and special miracles by Paul. Peter brought deliverance to the palsied Aeneas and life to the beloved Dorcas who had died. Acts 9:32-42. Peter also performed special miracles when his very shadow brought healing to those upon whom it fell. Acts 5:12-16.

A MIRACLE DEFINED

A miracle is an orderly intervention in the regular operations of nature: a supernatural suspension of a natural law. When Elisha made the iron to swim he reversed the law of nature which makes heavy objects sink. 2 Kings 6:1-7. Isaiah turned back the sundial of Ahaz ten degrees, as a sign to Hezekiah. Isa. 38:7, 8. Aaron cast down his rod before Pharaoh, and it became a serpent. Ex. 7:10. He smote the waters that were in the river, and they were turned to blood. v. 20. These were miracles.

INSTANCES OF MIRACLES

By his rod and his hand, Moses performed great miracles in Egypt and smote the Red Sea and it opened, a dry path, for the Children of Israel. Ex. 14: 16, 21. He cast a tree into the bitter waters of Marah to make them sweet. Ex. 15:23-25. He smote the rock to give water to the Israelites (Ex. 17:6); and held up his rod for victory over the Amalekites at Rephidim. Ex. 17:8-13. He was invited to exercise the gift of faith in speaking to the rock of Meribah-Kadesh (Num. 20:8), but rather, he exercised the gift of miracles and smote the rock to bring water. The Lord chided him with "because ye believed me not." v. 12. Elisha took the mantle of Elijah and smote the waters of Jordan to go over on dry ground. He cast salt into the spring of waters at Jericho and healed the waters. 2 Kings 2:19-22. He cast meal in the pottage in which there was death and there was no harm in the pot. 2 Kings 4:38-41.

RELATION OF MIRACLES TO THE HOLY SPIRIT BAPTISM AND TO CHRIST

The word "dunamis," which is translated "miracles" in 1 Cor. 12:10, is the same word which is translated "power" in Acts 1:8 ("Ye shall receive power, the Holy Ghost coming upon you"), and in Luke 24:49 ("until ye be undued with power from on high"). Christ is the power (dunamis) of God (1 Cor. 1:24), and He has promised to work with us confirming the word with signs following. Matt. 28:20; Mark 16:20. "Verily, verily I say unto you, He that believeth on me, the works that I do shall he do also: and greater works than these shall he do; because I go unto my Father." John 14:12. It is in fulfillment of this promise and in full realization of the promise of power in connection with the Baptism of the Spirit, that the gift of workings of miracles is given to the church.

SOVEREIGN MIRACLES

There are certain miracles recorded in the Bible which were God's sovereign works, not the result of either the gift of faith or the gift of the workings of miracles. When God first told Moses to cast his rod to the ground, it became a serpent, and Moses fled from it. At the command of God he put forth his hand and took it by the tail and it became a rod again. He thrust his hand into his bosom at God's command and it became leprous. He put it in again and it became as his other flesh. Ex. 4:2-7. God intervened for the protection of Daniel in the lions' den. It is not recorded or implied that Daniel spoke them into docility. God spoke from heaven and it was done. His presence with the three Hebrew children in the burning fiery furnace preserved them from destruction. The quality in Daniel and his companions which stands out here is their courage and utter consecration. "Our God . . . is able to deliver us, . . . but if not . . . " Daniel 3:17, 18. God commanded the ravens to feed Elijah by the brook

Cherith. 1 Kings 17:4. God sent the earthquake to deliver Paul and Silas when they were in prison, and opened the prison doors for Peter. Acts 16:26; 12:10. The Lord wrought the miracle of healing by a look at the uplifted serpent. Numbers 21:8. Again, the Lord whisked Philip away to a distant city in a moment of time. Acts 8:39, 40. Ezekiel also was carried by the Spirit to a distant point. Ezekiel 8:3. The Lord said unto Moses, "Behold I will rain bread from heaven for you." Exodus 16:4. And He is ever able to set a table for us in the wilderness, and do wonders on behalf of His children. His very name is Wonderful. Isaiah 9:6.

CHAPTER XXI

The Gift of Prophecy

GIFTS OF UTTERANCE

"YE abound in everything, in faith, and utterance, and knowledge." 2 Cor. 8:7. We have considered the gifts of revelation and power. We have now to consider the gifts of utterance. These gifts include prophecy, tongues, and interpretation of tongues. They all have to do with speaking and so are grouped together and called *the gifts of utterance*. They operate in the realm of the spirit. The gifts of utterance can be said to express and convey the emotions of God. The gifts of revelation express His mind, the gifts of power express His power, while the gifts of utterance give expression to the feelings of His heart.

THE WORDS OF GOD

Peter says, "If any man speak (gifts of utterance), let him speak as the oracles (word, *logos*) of God." 1 Peter 4:11. Let him speak as a mystic oracle—speak the very words of God, serve as an expression of the very mind of God, as Christ the Word is an expression of God. John 1:1, 18. How high and holy is such an expression and ministry!

THE EXPRESSION OF THE SPIRIT

Since prophecy was an expression of man's having received the Spirit's fullness in the Old Testament, and tongues is the evidence of the Baptism in the Spirit after Pentecost, it is clear that utterance is a logical, spontaneous outflow and expression of the Spirit. These are the gifts which noticeably characterize the Pentecostal Movement today.

PROPHECY THE GREATEST GIFT

The gift of prophecy is the only gift that we are told especially to covet. 1 Cor. 14:1, 39. It therefore must be considered as outranking in value and importance all the other gifts. A possible reason for the precedence given this gift is that through its medium the other best gifts find expression. Wisdom must be voiced or else it remains unused and latent. Prophecy is the voice through which wisdom speaks. Faith is the word of authority and must be spoken to be effective. Prophecy is the voice by which faith speaks. And prophecy has a function all its own as well. It is the voice of the Holy Spirit.

THE VOICE OF THE HOLY SPIRIT

"When the Comforter is come, . . . he shall testify of me." John 15:26. The Holy Ghost testifies and speaks, as He gives utterance to those who accept Him in His fullness. Acts 2:4. He uses human channels, human voices that are yielded to Him. As great omnipotent, omniscient Leader of the Church, He would naturally and properly desire and deserve opportunity to speak to His people. The gift of prophecy among Spirit-filled people affords Him that opportunity.

PROPHECY DEFINED

To prophesy means "to speak for another." Moses had demurred at God's calling him to speak to the Israelites and to Pharaoh, so God gave him Aaron to speak for him. "See I have made thee a god to Pharaoh; and Aaron thy brother shall be thy *prophet.*" Exodus 7:1. John the Baptist, the greatest of prophets, was a voice crying in the wilderness. Isaiah 40:3; Matt. 3:3; 11:9. Also prophecy can be defined as "speaking one's own language in the power of the Holy Spirit," or as "divine ability to forth-tell as well as to fore-tell."

THE ELEMENTS OF PROPHECY

"But he that prophesieth speaketh unto men to edification, and exhortation, and comfort." "He that prophesieth edifieth the church." "For ye may all prophesy one by one, that all may learn, and all may be comforted." 1 Cor. 14:3, 4, 31. The Holy Spirit wants to edify, exhort, comfort, and cause to learn; and He uses a yielded prophet through whom to accomplish these ends.

Edification.

Jesus said, "I will build my church." Matt.

[154]

16:18. The Holy Spirit has been given the contract of building the church. To edify is to build, and the Holy Spirit uses the New Testament prophet as a voice through which to do His work of building the church. There are two ways in which to build the church; add new material (new members) and to strengthen that which has already been added. "But if all prophesy, and there come in one that believeth not, or one unlearned, he is convinced of all, he is judged of all; and thus are the secrets of his heart made manifest; and so falling down on his face he will worship God, and report that God is in you of a truth." 1 Cor. 14:24, 25. Thus are converts added, and the church is built up. Tearing down or stumbling or driving people away is the exact opposite of the work of the Holy Spirit in prophecy, and that which produces this destructive result is not of the Holy Spirit. To build up the saints in the most holy faith (Jude 20) is to construct a holy temple in the Lord, "in whom ye also are builded together for an habitation of God through the Spirit." Eph. 2:21-22. To strengthen the saints, to increase their faith, and to develop their Christian character is the legitimate end and objective of the Holy Spirit as He speaks through one in the gift of prophecy.

Exhortation.

Exhortation is such a distinctive phase of the gift of prophecy that it is dignified by being called a gift itself. Romans 12:8. Here is the emotional

[155]

appeal characteristic of the gifts of utterance, not just an emotional outburst by way of relief for pent-up feelings, but a controlled stream of earnest, vibrant Holy Spirit words directed to sinner or saint with a plea to turn from wrong to right, from error to truth, to obedience and faith. God loves and God pleads, through the gift of prophecy.

Comfort.

Jesus gave us one of the major names of the Holy Spirit, the Comforter. John 14:16, 26. Since this is His very name, it is no wonder that one of His gifts has, as its definite end, the comfort of the saints. "That all may be comforted." 1 Cor. 14:31. The Lord loves His children and pours in His sympathy and His encouragement. He tells of His second coming ("things to come," John 16:13) that we may be comforted with those words. 1 Thess. 4:16-18. How sweet and encouraging the words of the Comforter as they are given to an Assembly through the lips of a godly speaker-of-prophecy.

PREDICTION

While it is not stated in 1 Cor. 14, that the gift of prophecy includes the ability to predict future events, it must not be overlooked that this element is inherent in a prophet's ministry. Much of the infallible prophecy of Scripture is devoted to foretelling. This is the glory of the God of Omniscience that He knows, and betimes discloses, the events of the future to and through His prophets. "When He is come,

. . . He will show you things to come." John 16:13.
It is true that events then unrevealed and future
have since been revealed to us by the infallible
writers of the New Testament, and hence this
function of the Spirit is no longer the most important. This explains why no reference is made to
it in 1 Corinthians 14.

EXAMPLES OF PREDICTION

But it must not be forgotten that there were
prophets in the early church who predicted as well
as gave messages for the present need. Agabus predicted that a dearth would come throughout all the
world, which came to pass in the days of Claudius
Caesar. Acts 11:27, 28. The Holy Spirit witnessed
in every city through which Paul passed on his way
to Jerusalem that bonds and afflictions awaited
him. Acts 20:23. Was not this prediction, and true
prediction? Agabus again predicted Paul's imprison-
ment at Jerusalem. Acts 21:10, 11. The element of
prediction, once so dominant in the gift of prophecy
that it gave that predominate meaning to the word
prophecy, is still inherent in this gift, although not
so necessary now to be exercised.

INFALLIBLE PROPHECY OF THE
SCRIPTURE

There are degrees of inspiration in prophecy.
Peter referred to "prophecy of the Scripture." 2
Peter 1:20. Jesus said, "One jot or one tittle shall
in no wise pass from the law, till all be fulfilled."

Matt. 5:18. "The Scripture cannot be broken." John 10:35. The prophecy of the Scriptures is infallible and there is neither flaw nor imperfection therein. "Not in the words which man's wisdom teacheth, but which the Holy Ghost teacheth." 1 Cor. 2:13.

FALLIBLE PROPHECY OF THE CHURCHES

But the operation of the gift of prophecy among the members of the Corinthian church and in churches today must be "judged." "Let the prophets speak two or three, and let the others judge." 1 Cor. 14:29. The reason for this is that it is possible for some to prophesy out of their own hearts and out of their own spirits. "Son of man, prophesy against the prophets of Israel that prophesy . . . out of their own hearts, Hear ye the word of the Lord: Thus saith the Lord God; Woe unto the foolish prophets, that follow their own spirit, and have seen nothing. . . . Therefore, behold, I am against you, saith the Lord God." Ezek. 13:2-8. How easy it is for one to allow one's own feelings or desires to enter into a message otherwise from God.

INSTANCES OF FALLIBLE PROPHECY

When Paul was on his final journey to Jerusalem, the Holy Spirit witnessed in every city that bonds and afflictions were awaiting him. Acts 20:23. At Tyre certain disciples said to Paul through the Spirit that he should not go up to Jerusalem. Acts 21:4. Agabus met them at Caesarea, "took Paul's girdle and bound his own hands and feet and said, Thus saith the Holy Ghost, So shall the Jews at Jerusalem bind the man that owneth this girdle." Acts 21:11. The disciples then tried to dissuade him from going, but he was determined to go. "And when he would not be persuaded, we ceased, saying, The will of the Lord be done." v. 14. Now let us "judge" these prophecies. The Holy Spirit witnessing in every city that bonds and afflictions abode him was right, for subsequent events proved it. Agabus was right. But the disciples at Tyre were partly right and partly wrong. That Paul would suffer was right, but that he should not go was their own desire and judgment. Paul accepted what was right and rejected the human in their message.

FALLIBLE PROPHECY AT THESSALONICA

Evidently there had been abuse of the gift of prophecy at Thessalonica. The prophets' messages were not appreciated and so the prophets had begun to quench the Spirit. Therefore Paul wrote, "Quench not the Spirit. Despise not prophesyings." But he did not say, "Accept all prophesying as the infallible word of God." But rather, "Prove all things; hold fast that which is good." 1 Thess. 5: 19-21.

WE SHOULD JUDGE MESSAGES

It is a false reverence which accepts everything which purports to be a divine message as if it were from God directly and without possible human admixture. "The simple believeth every word: but the prudent man looketh well to his going." Prov. 14:15. "Beloved, believe not every spirit, but try the spirits." 1 John 4:1. To the Corinthians and to all, Paul says, "Brethren, be not children in understanding; however in malice be ye children, but in understanding be men." 1 Cor. 14:20. This also applies to tongues and their interpretation (which together are equivalent to prophecy). Let us not allow our acceptance of tongues and prophecy in our churches (forbidding not to speak with tongues) run to the extreme of magnifying these gifts beyond their Scriptural value or position.

RULE FOR JUDGING MESSAGES

The way to judge or prove the manifestations of the gifts which appear in our churches is to estimate whether or not they are exhortation in nature, and result in edification and comfort to the believers. *The reception which is accorded the operation of the gift is the revelation and proof of its purity.* There is also the clear instruction, "If any man speak in an unknown tongue, let it be by two, or at the most by three, and that by course (in turn); and let one interpret. But if there be no interpreter, let him keep silence in the church: and let him speak to himself, and to God. Let the prophets speak two or three, and let the other judge." 1 Cor. 14:27-29. Disobedience to this regulation should be disapproved and judged to be wrong, for these "are the commandments of the Lord." v. 37.

GIFTS SUBJECT TO PERSONAL CONTROL

This leads logically to the scripture, "And the spirits of the prophets are subject to the prophets." 1 Cor. 14:32. "Prophets can control their own prophetic spirit" (Moffatt). This information is good for prophets to have, lest they think they are compelled or obligated to yield to all spirit impulses that come to them. It is not quenching the Spirit to be guided by our knowledge of Scriptural regulation, by our respect for senior officers in the church, and by our love for others in exercising our gifts.

PROPHECY NOT FOR GUIDANCE

There is no case on Scriptural record where prophecy, or tongues, was used as a means of guidance or discovery of the will of God. At the time of the greatest crisis in the early church, when apostles, elders, and brethren came together to consider the matter of circumcision being essential to salvation, no message in prophecy or tongues and interpretation was given to decide the matter. As already seen, when Paul was en route to Jerusalem, he rejected the effort of well-meaning friends who tried to prophesy as a means of guidance. Acts 21:4, 14. It was a vision in the night that Paul took as God's invitation for him to go into Macedonia, rather than a message by the prophet Silas who was his companion. Acts 16:9, 10. The word of wisdom is the gift which we can expect to function when personal or church guidance is needed, rather than the gift of prophecy or tongues and interpretation.

[161]

CHAPTER XXII

Tongues and Interpretation of Tongues

GOD CREATED GIFT OF TONGUES

IT has been stated that tongues plus interpretation equal prophecy. This is based on 1 Cor. 14:5, and is true. Why then is there such a thing as the gift of tongues when prophecy, in the plan of God, gives directly in one's own language the message of the Spirit? The first answer is that which God has done is always well done, and it is not becoming of us to criticize God. Isaiah prophesied by the Spirit, "For with stammering lips and another tongue will he speak to this people." Isa. 28: 11, 12. Jesus Himself said, "And these signs shall follow them that believe; . . . they shall speak with new tongues." Mark 16:17. Thus, tongues are God's idea and operation, and they who criticize Him and His plan do so at their own peril.

THIS GIFT INDICATES LOVE FOR *ALL* NATIONS

We can also see some of the reasons why God has given the gift of tongues and the gift of interpretation, in additon to the gift of prophecy to which they are equivalent. As has been pointed out in the chapter on the "Evidence of the Baptism in the Spirit," before the day of Pentecost, when salvation was of one nation (the Jews), the mother tongue was sufficient as a vehicle for the Spirit's message. But on the day of Pentecost, salvation became available to all people and nations, so other and many tongues are now chosen by the Spirit as the vehicle through which to speak. The change of language through which He speaks at the time of His incoming is significant and indicative of the fact that now He wants His message to go to all nations, to the ends of the earth. Matt. 28:19; Acts 1:8.

PENTECOST VERSUS BABEL

Going back still farther into Old Testament history for our antecedent, what do we find is the relation between the speaking with tongues on the day of Pentecost and the confusion of tongues at the tower of Babel? For one thing, we see that God long ago displayed His power to give men (even rebellious men) another tongue and language, and to give it to them as a permanent gift. Why should it be thought a thing incredible that the Lord could give to His own disciples the ability to speak His praise in an unknown or unlearned tongue as the Spirit gives utterance? In addition to that, the tongues at Pentecost were an indication and a hint that it was God's purpose ultimately to undo the confusion and separation which came at the tower of Babel and bring together in one the children of God that were scattered abroad. John 11:52.

TONGUES FOR A SIGN

"In the law it is written, With men of other tongues and other lips will I speak unto this people; and yet for all that will they not hear me, saith the Lord. Wherefore tongues are for a sign . . . to them that believe not." 1 Cor. 14:21, 22. On the day of Pentecost "devout men, out of every nation under heaven . . . came together and were confounded because that every man heard them speak in his own language. And they were all amazed and marveled, saying one to another, Behold, are not all these which speak Galilaeans? And how hear we every man in our own tongue, wherein we were born? . . . We do hear them speak in our tongues the wonderful works of God." Acts 2:5-11. They had not yet heard Peter's preaching to them. He preached to them later in their own language. But they had overheard the disciples as they were filled with the Spirit and spoke with other tongues as the Spirit gave them utterance. On this occasion tongues were a most convincing sign to unbelievers. There have been many other occasions since when this has happened, for tongues are set "for a sign."

TONGUES FOR PRAYER

It is stated in 1 Cor. 14 that the chief use of tongues is in prayer. "For he that speaketh in an unknown tongue speaketh not unto man, but unto God: for no man understandeth him; howbeit in the Spirit he speaketh mysteries." v. 2. "For if I pray in an unknown tongue, my spirit prayeth, but my understanding is unfruitful. What is it then? I will pray with the Spirit, and I will pray with the understanding also." vv. 14, 15. The saints who love their Lord the most and who thrill to the delights of prayer will enter into the sentiments of Charles Wesley who sighed, "Oh, for a thousand tongues to sing my Great Redeemer's praise!" The gift of tongues is the answer to their prayer and deep heart-desire. The Spirit has provided the tongues of men and of angels with which to pour out our hearts to God. "Likewise the Spirit also helpeth our infirmities: for we know not what we should pray for as we ought: but the Spirit himself maketh intercession for us with groanings which cannot be uttered." Romans 8:26. Tongues are a God-ordained outlet through which the Spirit of Supplications will let His petitions ascend to the heavenly throne. They are needed in the plan of God.

TONGUES FOR MESSAGES

Another purpose and use of the gift of tongues is as a vehicle of expression for messages to the church. Tongues without interpretation, in the church, Paul explains at great length, are meaningless and thus

out of order. 1 Cor. 14:5-13, 16-20, 23, 27, 28
(17 verses). The speaker in tongues should pray
that he himself might interpret and, in all cases,
should keep silent if there is no interpreter present.
Also there should not be more than three messages
in tongues during a service. But these regulations
were not intended to be strangulations. If tongues
with interpretation equals prophecy, and if Peter
called the tongues on the day of Pentecost the fulfillment of Joel's prophecy, "I will pour out My
Spirit upon all flesh and they shall *prophesy*," then
we can consider that tongues (with interpretation)
should have the same effect and result in a church
meeting that prophecy has; namely, edification, exhortation, and comfort. "When ye be come together, every one of you hath a psalm, hath a
doctrine, hath a tongue, hath a revelation, hath an
interpretation. Let all things be done unto edifying."
v. 26. This is when the whole church is come together in one place. v. 23. Tongues is one of the
manifestations of the Spirit which are given to
profit withal. 1 Cor. 12:7. "Wherefore brethren, . . .
forbid not to speak with tongues." v. 39.

INTERPRETATION OF TONGUES DEFINED

The interpretation of tongues has been referred
to many times in the treatment of the gift of tongues.
A few additional comments, therefore, concerning
this gift may suffice. Interpretation of tongues has
nothing to do with the interpretation of Scripture.
That is the work of the teacher. Interpretation of

tongues is a supernatural gift, like the gift of tongues or the gift of miracles. It is entirely dependent upon the gift of tongues and has no function apart from that gift. It is in reality an interpreting or giving the sense of that which has been spoken in the gift of tongues.

THE NATURE OF THIS GIFT

The interpreter of tongues, who also speaks as the Spirit gives utterance, need not give a word-for-word exact translation of the message in tongues. The word translated "interpret" used here means "to explain thoroughly, to give the sense and the significance." "He expounded (the same word translated "interpret" in 1 Cor. 12 and 14) unto them in all the Scriptures the things concerning himself." Luke 24:27. This more accurately expresses to us the idea of explaining thoroughly and carefully the full meaning. This then is the nature of the gift of interpretation. The message in tongues may be short and a much longer interpretation ensue, and vice versa. When Daniel interpreted the three words which Belshazzar saw written on the wall, he used three sentences in which to give the interpretation. Daniel 5:25-28. He explained the meaning of the words to the king.

ITS IMPORTANCE

Let him who has the gift of interpretation consider the importance of his gift. The speaker-in-tongues is dependent upon the interpreter for the completion

[167]

of his message. If the latter fails, the message in tongues has been given in vain, the time of the assembly wasted, and the Scriptures disobeyed. The responsibility for this failure rests upon the interpreter if he has quenched the Spirit. "Quench not the Spirit." Also the quality of the message in tongues will be judged by the interpretation, for the interpretation is all that is understandable to the hearers. The message must be to edification, exhortation, or to comfort; and Spirit-filled Christians present will be able to sense whether or not the message has served to this end. By the spiritual quality and Scriptural correctness of the interpretation both the message and its interpretation will be judged.

CHAPTER XXIII

The Holy Spirit in the Church—General

SCRIPTURE HISTORY OF THE HOLY SPIRIT RESUMED

IN our study of the Holy Spirit, we have considered His part in the Trinity, His Personality, and His Deity. His nature and general ministry have been revealed by a study of His names. The history of the Holy Spirit also has been studied, beginning in the Old Testament and continuing through the Life of Christ. At that point we turned aside from chronological sequence to study the Holy Spirit in the conversion of the believer, the Baptism in the Holy Spirit, and the Gifts of the Spirit. We now return to take up the sequence in the history of the Holy Spirit and begin to study the Holy Spirit in the Church.

THE ADVENT OF THE SPIRIT

The prophets in the Old Testament and Jesus and

John during their lifetime prophesied that the Holy Spirit would come to the earth in a special way at a certain time. These prophecies were fulfilled on that great day of Pentecost which followed Christ's Passover offering for the sins of the world. "And when the day of Pentecost was fully come, they were all with one accord in one place. And suddenly there came a sound from heaven as of a rushing mighty wind, and it filled all the house where they were sitting. And there appeared unto them cloven tongues like as of fire, and it sat upon each of them. And they were all filled with the Holy Ghost, and began to speak with other tongues, as the Spirit gave them utterance." Acts 2:1-4. This is the description of the advent of the Spirit.

LIKE CHRIST'S FIRST ADVENT

As angels heralded the birth of the Savior and a star guided the Wise Men to His bed, so the "birth of the Holy Spirit" on the earth, so to speak, in this dispensation was marked by its own phenomena. Christ was the Creator of this earth at the beginning. "Before Abraham was, I am," He said. John 8:58. He revealed Himself in the Old Testament at certain times. Yet there was a specific time when He was born on this earth. "A body hast thou prepared me" (Heb. 10:5), and He came to indwell that body and spend a period of life and ministry on this earth, later to be received back into heaven. In like manner the Holy Spirit was present and operative in the Old Testament. But up until the last year

[170]

of Christ's life on earth, John reported, "The Holy Ghost was not yet given; because that Jesus was not yet glorified." John 7:39. But He did come in all His regal splendor on the Day of Pentecost. As the birth of the Babe at Bethlehem was the advent of Christ, so the descent of the Holy Spirit on the Day of Pentecost was the advent of the Holy Spirit. As Christmas is the celebration of the birthday of Christ, so Pentecost is the birthday of the Holy Spirit. "Augustine calls the day of Pentecost the 'dies natilis' [natal day] of the Holy Ghost; and for the same reason that the day when Mary brought forth her first-born son we name 'the birthday of Jesus Christ.' " [1]

HE FILLS HIS TEMPLE

Not as a helpless babe does the Holy Spirit come to this earth. There are no thirty years to wait until He begins His ministry. Instantly He occupies the body which Christ had prepared Him—the 120 waiting disciples—and fills them with His glory. When Solomon had prepared the temple for Jehovah's incoming of old, 120 priests sounded with trumpets and "it came even to pass, as the trumpeters and singers were as one, to make one sound to be heard in praising and thanking the Lord; and when they lifted up their voice with the trumpets and cymbals and instruments of musick, and praised

---

[1] A. J. Gordon, *The Ministry of the Spirit* (Fleming Revell, New York, [1894]), p. 19.

the Lord, saying, For He is good; for His mercy
endureth forever; that then the house was filled
with a cloud, even the house of the Lord; so that
the priests could not stand to minister by reason of
the cloud; for the glory of the Lord had filled the
house of God." 2 Chron. 5:13-14.   The Spirit's
coming on the day of Pentecost was similar. The
120 disciples were of one accord and had made one
sound in praising the Lord, and then the house
where they were sitting was filled with the sound of
a rushing mighty wind and the bodies of the disciples
themselves, as temples, were filled with the Holy
Spirit. And they could not stand upright to minister,
for the mockers said, "These men are full of new
wine." Acts 2:13.

HE BEGINS HIS MINISTRY

Immediately the Holy Spirit began His ministry.
He testified (John 15:26) through all of the infilled disciples. Knowing all languages and knowing
the nationalities who were present at Jerusalem on
that feast day, and desiring to win their souls for
the Body of Christ, He began to speak in those
languages to them. They were amazed as they heard
in their own tongue the wonderful works of God,
and asked, What meaneth this? They were thus prepared for Peter's message in the power of the Holy
Spirit, and were pricked in their hearts by the Holy
Spirit. Three thousand souls were won and added to
the Lord, to His mystic body, in that first day's
work of the Holy Spirit. He empowered Peter and

John with the gift of faith which enabled them to heal the man at the Gate Beautiful and to bring the people together greatly wondering. Again Peter preached in the power of the Spirit, and many which heard the Word believed, the number of the men being about five thousand. Acts 4:4.

HIS MINISTRY CONTINUES

The Holy Spirit stood with Peter and infilled him as he stood before the Sanhedrin and testified boldly that there was none other name under heaven, whereby men could be saved. Acts 4:8-12. He came again upon the praying disciples and the place was shaken where they were gathered together. Acts 4:31. His holiness was not to be trifled with by the deceiving Ananias and Sapphira and they were stricken dead. His eyes saw their sin through the eyes of Peter and He rebuked them through Peter's mouth. When the apostles were once more arrested, He sent His angel and released them from prison. Peter again spoke boldly and declared that not only they were witnesses of Christ but that the Holy Spirit also was a witness. Acts 5:32. The deacons were full of the Holy Spirit, and the Spirit was filling Stephen in the hour of his martyrdom.

HE OPERATES THROUGH THE CHURCH

And on through the book which should be called "The Acts of the Holy Ghost," He dominates the scene. Through and with Peter and John, Stephen, Philip, Paul, Barnabas, Silas, Agabus and others, the Holy Spirit is the invisible Other Comforter who has taken Christ's place as teacher and leader among His disciples. At the Council at Jerusalem (Acts 15), at the church at Antioch (Acts 13), and at all similar deliberations, He administers the affairs of the Church through the gifts of government. 1 Cor. 12:28. From the original visitation to the parent church at Jerusalem (Acts 2) ; on through similar visitations to the churches, at Samaria (Acts 8) ; at Caesarea (Acts 10) ; at Antioch in Syria (Acts 13:2) ; at Antioch in Pisidia (Acts 13:52) ; in Galatia (Gal 3:2;) in Ephesus (Acts 19:1-7) ; and at Corinth (1 Cor. 12:13) ; the Holy Spirit personally infills the believers. As Christ could not do when He was here in the flesh, the Spirit now indwells the bodies of these yielded believers and works through them the mighty works and words of power, which He wrought in Christ during Christ's visible presence here on earth. A very real Commander in Chief leads on to victory.

A TRIUMPHANT ONE-GENERATION VICTORY

This was the secret of the phenomenal success of the early church. They were ignorant and unlearned men. Acts 4:13.   Silver and gold had they none. Acts 3:6. Their church machinery was very simple: apostles, elders, deacons, prophets, and teachers, bound together chiefly by ties of love and a common purpose. They had no prestige, for they were made as the filth of the world and the offscouring of all things (1 Cor. 4:13); they were the sect that was everywhere spoken against. Acts 28:22. And yet, they turned the world upside down. Acts 17:6. The gospel was preached in all the world and to every creature under heaven. Col. 1:6, 23. Churches were established in every land. The whole secret and explanation is the fact that the apostles and new disciples were filled with the Holy Spirit. The Holy Spirit was honored and given leadership and control over their bodies and whole lives. He was immanent and dominant. He indwelt His workers with power; He invested them with His gifts. He went with them to prison, to the martyr's stake, and to the whipping post. They went with Him and He with them. Yea, they took Him and He took them. Together, the Holy Spirit and His body (which is the Body of Christ) went on to the amazing victory of the Apostolic days.

CHAPTER XXIV

The Holy Spirit in the Church—Local

THE church universal consists of many local units. The Holy Spirit dwells in the church at large and He also dwells in each individual church. There is an ordained manner of operation for each local church under the power and control of the Holy Spirit. It is this phase of the presence and work of the Holy Spirit in the church which we shall consider in this chapter.

HE DRAWS THE SAINTS TOGETHER

"By one Spirit are we all baptized into one body, ... and have all been made to drink into one Spirit." 1 Cor. 12:13. "Now ye are the body of Christ and members in particular." v. 27. This intimate, vital relationship makes Christians one with each other in a sense that no lodge or fraternity can bind men together. Here is organism, as well as organization; unity, as well as union. This Spirit relationship draws us to each other as a magnet draws pieces of steel—"not forsaking the assembling of ourselves together." Heb. 10:25. We are together in Christ. We are together in the Holy Spirit. It is logical and inevitable that we should seek to assemble ourselves together constantly.

ORDER OF WORSHIP

When the whole church be come together in one place, then what is the Scriptural procedure? "Every one of you hath a psalm, hath a doctrine, hath a tongue, hath a revelation, hath an interpretation." 1 Cor. 14:26. "Exhort one another." Heb. 3:13. "Comfort one another." 1 Thess. 4:18. "Teaching and admonishing one another in psalms and hyms and spiritual songs." Col. 3:16. "Confess your sins one to another." James 5:16. R.V. "Pray one for another." James 5:16. "Love one another." 1 Peter 1:22. "Bear ye one another's burdens." Gal. 6:2. Here is congregational worship at its purest. Every member of the body participating. "For ye may *all* prophesy one by one, that all may learn, and all be comforted." "I would that ye *all* spake with tongues, but rather that ye prophesied." 1 Cor. 14: 5, 31. The whole body animated, inspired, and indwelt by the Holy Spirit and yielded to His operation.

[177]

THE HOLY SPIRIT PROVIDES WORKERS AND OPERATES THROUGH THEM

"God hath set some in the church, first apostles, secondarily prophets, thirdly teachers, after that miracles, then gifts of healings, helps, governments, diversities of tongues." 1 Cor. 12:28. "Wherefore he saith, when he ascended up on high, . . . he gave gifts unto men." "And he gave some apostles; and some, prophets; and some, evangelists; and some, pastors and teachers; for the perfecting of the saints, for (or unto) the work of the ministry, for the edifying of the body of Christ." Eph. 4:8, 11, 12. As this is true of the church universal, so to some extent it must be true of local churches. In them, too, should appear the ministry of apostles, prophets, evangelists, pastors, and teachers. Also there should occur healings, tongues, and Spirit-led business meetings. All of these function in the power of the Holy Spirit operating in one or more of the gifts of the Spirit. This is the kind of ministry that is ordained of God.

HOLY SPIRIT PREACHING

Preaching with wisdom of words, with enticing words of man's wisdom, or with excellency of speech which is purely natural, is as much an intrusion of the profane into the holy as an admission of a Canaanite into the house of the Lord of Hosts. Zech. 14:21. Paul preached with the Holy Spirit gift of the Word of Wisdom, and dared not preach otherwise. 1 Cor. 1 and 2. "For our gospel came not unto you in word only, but also in power, and in the Holy Ghost, and in much assurance." 1 Thess. 1:5. And let the word be received with joy of the Holy Ghost as it was at Thessalonica. 1 Thess. 1:6. Peter also speaks of preaching the gospel unto you with the Holy Ghost sent down from heaven. 1 Peter 1:12. This is the kind of preaching that results in what Peter experienced at Cornelius' household, when "The Holy Ghost fell on all them which heard the word." Acts 10:44.

HOLY SPIRIT SINGING

"Be filled with the Spirit, speaking to yourselves in psalms and hymns and spiritual songs, singing and making melody in your heart to the Lord." Eph. 5:18-19. Paul says, "I will sing with (or in) the Spirit, and I will sing with the understanding also." 1 Cor. 14:15. Here is spiritual, Holy Spirit singing. It is the outflow of the Spirit-filled experience. It is "to the Lord." Not to the audience, but to the Lord. What room is there here for the unconverted to participate? How can the "world" receive the Spirit and function as a member of the body of Christ, as that body unites in singing God's praises? It is a violation and a desecration of the holy place for the unconverted to stand on the sacred rostrum for ministry in word or song. Let the high praises of God be in our mouths. "Bless the Lord, O my soul; and all that is within me, bless His holy name." Psalm 103:1. How better can we praise our God than with the Spirit of Praise whom He has

[179]

given us? All who are filled with the Spirit should yield to the Spirit of Praise and submit themselves one to another in the fear of God as together they speak to themselves in psalms and hymns and spiritual songs, singing and making melody in their hearts to the Lord. Eph. 5:19, 21. This is the Bible's emphasis on Spirit-filled congregational singing. Let us beware lest our so-called "special" singing degenerate into a carnal display of human talents or purely natural entertainment.

"PRAYING IN THE HOLY GHOST"

Collective or public prayer is a vital part of public worship. The Holy Spirit stands ready to take control of yielded vessels and pray through them as the Spirit of Supplications. No one knows better than He that for which we ought to pray. As we yield our thoughts and our tongues, He will pray through us according to the will of God. Rom. 8:26,27. When Paul commands that we pray always with all prayer and supplication *in the Spirit,* he meant pray *in the Spirit.* Eph. 6:18. Jude refers to the same experience when he says, "Praying in the Holy Ghost." Jude 20. It is at this point when the believer and the church face heavenward, acknowledge God as the Source of all blessing, thank Him for those blessings, bless God and minister unto Him, offering incense (which is the prayers of the saints, Rev. 5:8; 8:3, 4). It is here that he and they need the interposition of the Holy Spirit. They that worship Him must worship Him in spirit and in

truth; for the Father seeketh such to worship Him.
John 4:23, 24. How can we better worship Him in
spirit than to worship Him in *the* Spirit, yielding
our voices to His utterance? "For through Him we
both have access *by one Spirit* unto the Father."
Eph. 2:18. In, by, and through the Holy Spirit,
we should pray unto the Father. All public as well as
private prayer should be God-anointed and Spirit-
energized.

CONCERTED PRAYING

A time set aside for a concert of spontaneous individual prayer should not be considered strange.
When Peter and John returned from their first
arrest and trial before the Sanhedrin, they reported
all that the chief priests and elders had said unto
them. "And when they heard that, *they lifted up
their voice to God with one accord* and said, Lord
thou art God," etc. Acts 4:24. Since worship should
be personal and individual, why should not all believers be given individual opportunity to pour
out their hearts to God in prayer? "And I heard as
it were the voice of a great multitude, and as the
voice of many waters, and as the voice of mighty
thunderings, saying, Alleluia: for the Lord God
omnipotent reigneth." Rev. 19:6. What is it then?
May there not be rehearsals on a small scale here, as
they are sincere and spontaneous? Why should only
the church have the stillness of a cemetery? This
is the quietest world in which men will ever live. The
wicked spend their eternity where there is weeping

and gnashing of teeth and the shrieks and moans of the damned. The redeemed join the angels in praising God with a loud voice. Rev. 5:8-12. And the living creatures rest not day and night, saying Holy, Holy, Holy, Lord God Almighty, which was, and is, and is to come. Rev. 4:8. And even in this world, in all other exercises, men are free to express their feelings and emotions. It is not a sin to feel, or to cry, or to laugh. And when feeling gets into religion and worship, it only proves that it is from the heart, the seat of the emotions.

PROPHESYING

Preaching, singing, and prayer do not exhaust possible exercises in a Spirit-filled church. "For ye may *all* prophesy"; "I would that ye *all* spake with tongues." 1 Cor. 14:5, 31. The speaking forth under the unction of the Holy Spirit (as the Spirit gives utterance) in a known or unknown tongue by the rank-and-file members of the church is God-ordained and should occur in our churches. "Despise not prophesyings"; "Forbid not to speak with tongues." 1 Thess. 5:20; 1 Cor. 14:39. It appears that in Paul's time, these gifts were abused and exercised to excess and that is why the Thessalonians had quenched the Spirit, and why Paul spoke so much about the regulation of these gifts in 1 Cor. 14. The Scriptural rule governing the operation of these gifts is that the prophets should speak one by one and not more than three in one service. v. 29. They who have the gift of tongues should likewise speak not more than three messages in one service, and the tongues should be interpreted. v. 27. These rules are mandatory. "If any man think himself to be a prophet or spiritual, let him acknowledge that the things that I write unto you are the commandments of the Lord." 1 Cor. 14:37. If the excess among the Corinthians was due to ignorance, what shall be said today of any disregard of these simple rules which are now written plainly? Let none of us transgress or cause the full Gospel to suffer by carelessness or disobedience in these matters.

LIFTING UP HOLY HANDS

There are, at times, demonstrations and manifestations which occur among Spirit-filled believers which are in marked contrast to the staid, still atmosphere of many modern churches. As saints in prayer or praise lift up their hands and reach out toward God, we have a demonstration which is considered unusual. But have you never read, "I will therefore that men pray everwhere, *lifting up holy hands*, without wrath and doubting"? 1 Timothy 2:8. And *"Lift up your hands* in the sanctuary and bless the Lord"? Psalm 134:2. And, "Let my prayer be set forth before thee as incense; and the *lifting up of my hands* as the evening sacrifice"? Psalm 141:2. The restoration of this beautiful expression of yearning and yielding toward God should be welcomed.

CLAPPING HANDS

The world's habit of clapping the hands by way

of applause is in reality an imitation of a holy practice. "O clap your hands, all ye people; shout unto God with the voice of triumph." Psalm 47:1. Speakers or singers should never be applauded in the house of God, for it is honoring the flesh and has no place in the worship of Jehovah. "How can ye believe which receive honor one of another, and seek not the honor which cometh from God only?" Jesus asked. John 5:44. He is a jealous God, and will not give His glory to another. "Do we provoke the Lord to jealousy? Are we stronger than he?" 1 Cor. 10:22. The house of God is the place to honor and worship God and God alone.

DANCING IN THE SPIRIT

The dance also has a holy function as an expression of joy. "Let them praise His name in the dance." Psalm 149:3. "Praise him with the timbrel and dance." Psalm 150:4. "David danced before the Lord with all his might." 2 Samuel 6:14. Michal, his wife, saw him and despised him in her heart; and upon his return home, she ridiculed him. David answered, "It was before the Lord, . . . therefore will I play before the Lord." God accepted David's method of praise and punished Michal. "Therefore Michal the daughter of Saul had no child unto the day of her death." 2 Samuel 6:23. Let modern Michals take note, and beware!

LOUD SHOUTING

Shouting aloud the praises of God is not foreign

to Scriptural worship. "Make a joyful noise unto the Lord, all the earth; make a loud noise, and rejoice, and sing praise." Psalm 98:4. "Shout unto God with the voice of triumph." Psalm 47:1. On Christ's triumphal entry into Jerusalem "the whole multitude of the disciples began to rejoice and praise God with a loud voice, for all the mighty works that they had seen. And some of the Pharisees from among the multitude said unto him, Master, rebuke thy disciples. And he answered and said unto them, I tell you that, if these should hold their peace, the stones would immediately cry out." Luke 19:37-40. Which shall we be: the Pharisees, or those who worship God with a loud voice?

PROSTRATION

The presence of the Lord can become so real and overwhelming that one falls prostrate at His feet. When Daniel saw his great vision, he said, "There remained no strength in me: for my comeliness was turned in me into corruption, and I retained no strength." Daniel 10:8. When John saw his vision on the isle of Patmos, he also fell at the Lord's feet as dead. Rev. 1:17. The Roman soldiers, when they saw the angel on the resurrection morning, "did shake, and became as dead men." Matt. 28:4. In heaven, too, they fall before Him in holy reverence. Rev. 4:10. It is a spontaneous and perfectly natural reaction to the glory of the Almighty God. Receiving the glorious baptism of the Holy Spirit is an occasion when many fall prostrate under the

[185]

power of God. Staid congregations still sing: "Oh, that with yonder sacred throng, we at His feet may fall; we'll join the everlasting song, and crown Him Lord of all." And, "At the name of Jesus, bowing, falling prostrate at His feet; King of kings in heaven we'll crown Him, when our journey is complete." Why this pious expression and expectation, with no entry now into that experience which honors God and brings overwhelming glory to one's soul?

LET ALL THINGS BE DONE TO EDIFY

It is not Scriptural or spiritual to suppress these emotional impulses if they are spontaneous and sincere, and are felt by those whose lives are pure and godly. On the other hand, they who worship God in the Spirit should carefully observe the Scriptural law governing all spiritual manifestations. They are given to profit withal. 1 Cor. 12:7. The gifts and operations of the Spirit are for the purpose of edifying the church. 1 Cor. 14:4, 5, 12, 17, 26. This is a good rule by which to judge all physical manifestations in the worship of Spirit-filled saints. Tongues, prophecy, wisdom, knowledge, faith, and great personal sacrifice are of no avail and as nothing, if they are not motivated by love. 1 Cor. 13. If the exercise of our gift or personal blessing does not edify the church and profit withal, love dictates that we remain silent and control our spirit and our blessing.

[186]

CHAPTER XXV

The Holy Spirit in the Future

FORMATION OF CHRIST'S BODY

AND when he is come, he will reprove the world of sin, and of righteousness, and of judgment." John 16:8. Through sanctification of the Spirit, men are brought to obedience and belief of the truth—to salvation. 2 Thess. 2:13. This is the work of the Holy Spirit in this dispensation: to seek, to find, to save, to sanctify, to baptize, and to gather out a people for His name. Acts 15:14. As these individuals are won and this company grows, the Holy Spirit indwells them. They are the temples of the Holy Spirit and become His body. 1 Cor. 3:16 (the church as a group) ; 1 Cor. 6:19 (individuals). This group is, of course, also the body of Christ. 1 Cor. 12:13, 14.

ASCENSION OF THAT BODY

At that time which is known to God alone, the Body of Christ shall have been completed, and the work of the Holy Spirit on earth during this dispensation shall have been finished. As the Spirit of life and glory within the church, the Holy Spirit will effect that transformation of the living Christians and resurrection of the dead in Christ which will comprise that glorious event, the rapture of the church. "But if the Spirit of Him that raised up Jesus from the dead dwell in you, he that raised up Christ from the dead shall also quicken your mortal bodies by His Spirit that dwelleth in you." Rom. 8:11. "Who shall change our vile body, that it may be fashioned like unto His glorious body, according to the working [of the Holy Spirit] whereby He is able even to subdue all things unto Himself." Phil. 3:21. "And so shall we ever be with the Lord." 1 Thess. 4:17.

INTO THE FULLNESS OF GLORY

This resurrection and translation of the saints has an extent of glory which we cannot comprehend. "Beloved, now are we the sons of God, and it doth not yet appear what we shall be." 1 John 3:2. We are told that we now have the earnest of the Spirit (2 Cor. 1:22; 5:5) and the first fruits of the Spirit. Rom. 8:23. We are sealed unto the day of redemption. Eph. 4:30. What does this mean? We have only a portion of Him and His power in our lives now. A small portion, too, since an earnest is always a small portion, and since the first fruits are few in comparison with the harvest. The time is coming when the Spirit will envelop us with His power, transform our bodies by His might, and transport us to glory. "Then shall be brought to pass the saying that is written, Death is swallowed up in victory." 1 Cor. 15:54. This will be the manifestation of the sons of God, the glorious liberty of the children of God. Rom. 8:19, 21. It will come at the time of the redemption of our bodies, the fullness of our adoption into the family of God. v. 23. This will be the triumphant climax to the work of the Holy Spirit in the church in this dispensation. "We shall be like him; for we shall see him as he is." 1 John 3:2.

THE HOLY SPIRIT'S WORK DURING THE TRIBULATION

After the Rapture of the Church, the Holy Spirit will deal particularly with the Jewish remnant, the 144,000 that are to be sealed by Him. Rev. 7:1-8. It may be that this is the time when it shall come to pass that "When the enemy shall come in like a flood, the Spirit of the Lord shall lift up a standard against Him." Isaiah 59:19. In the last part of the tribulation, the Lord will pour upon the house of David, and upon the inhabitants of Jerusalem, the spirit of grace and of supplications, "and they shall look upon Him whom they have pierced." Zech. 12:10. Thus the Holy Spirit effects the conversion of a nation in a day. Isa. 66:7, 8.

THE HOLY SPIRIT'S WORK DURING THE MILLENNIUM

As our present baptism in the Spirit, walk in the

Spirit, and knowledge of the Spirit are but a fore-taste of the fullness which awaits us at the coming of our Lord and Savior, so the whole work and ministry of the Spirit on the earth in this dispensation are but drops of blessing compared with the great, sweeping universal work that is before Him during the Millennium. Christ in person and the Holy Spirit in immanent presence work hand in hand in the reclamation and transformation of the earth in this period. With the removal from the earth, at Armageddon, of all who had taken the mark of the beast during the tribulation the binding of Satan in the bottomless pit, the return to this earth of the redeemed of all ages who will constitute the Bride of Christ reigning at His side, the Holy Spirit will then have full and free sway among the sons of men. Then shall Joel's prophecy find its full fulfillment: "It shall come to pass afterward (in the last days, Acts 2:17) that I will pour out my Spirit upon all flesh." Joel 2:28, 29. Isaiah also wrote of this time when "the Spirit be poured upon us from on high." Isa. 32:15. Also in Isa. 44:3: "For I will pour water upon him that is thirsty, and floods upon the dry ground: I will pour my Spirit upon thy seed, and my blessing upon thine offspring." Ezekiel adds his prophecy (36: 27): "And I will put my Spirit within you and cause you to walk in my statutes."

THE ULTIMATE TRIUMPH

These are the days when "The eyes of the blind

shall be opened, and the ears of the deaf shall be unstopped. Then shall the lame man leap as an hart, and the tongue of the dumb sing: for in the wilderness shall waters break out, and streams in the desert." "And the inhabitant shall not say, I am sick." Isa. 35: 5, 6; 33:24. "The earth shall be full of the knowledge of the Lord, as the waters cover the sea." Isa. 11:9. "For from the rising of the sun unto the going down of the same, my name shall be great among the Gentiles; and in every place incense shall be offered unto my name, and a pure offering: for my name shall be great among the heathen, saith the Lord of hosts." Mal. 1:11. "He shall have dominion also from sea to sea, and from the river unto the ends of the earth." Psalm 72:8. "And they shall teach no more every man his neighbor, and every man his brother, saying, Know the Lord: for they shall all know me, from the least of them unto the greatest of them, saith the Lord." Jer. 31: 34. This will be the grand climax of the work of the Holy Spirit. To pervade the earth with His presence, to teach men to glorify the Lord, to drive out all sickness, to deliver the groaning creation itself, and to bring all things into subjection to Christ—these are His great objectives, and the thousand years of peace will witness His complete attainment of these great ends.

BIBLIOGRAPHY

Baxter, Mrs. M., *Holy Ghost Days,* London, Christian Herald Office.

Brumback, Carl, *What Meaneth This?* Springfield, Mo., Gospel Publishing House.

Cumming, J. Elder, D.D., *Through the Eternal Spirit,* London, Drummond Tract Depot, 1937.

Frodsham, S. H., *With Signs Following,* Springfield, Missouri, Gospel Publishing House.

Gardiner, F. Stuart, M.A., *The Power of the Spirit,* New York, Charles Scribner Sons.

Gee, Donald, *Concerning Spiritual Gifts,* Springfield, Missouri, Gospel Publishing House.

Goforth, Jonathan, D.D., *By My Spirit,* New York, Harper Brothers.

Gordon, A. J., D.D., *Ministry of Healing,* Harrisburg, Pa., Christian Publications Incorporated.
Ministry of the Spirit, Philadelphia, American Baptist Publishing Society, 1896.

Greenfield, John, *Power From on High.*

Henry, Matthew, *Commentaries,* New York, Revell.

Hopkins, *Law of Liberty.*

Kelley, Wm., *Lectures on the New Testament Doctrine of the Holy Spirit.*

Lawson, J. Gilchrist, *Deeper Experiences of Famous Christians.*

McIntire, Rev. James R., *The Life of the Holy Spirit,* St. Louis, Bethany Press, 1930.

McNeil, John, *Spirit-Filled Life.*

McQuilkin, Robt. C., *What Is Pentecost's Message Today?* Philadelphia, Sunday School Times.

Mahan, A., *Baptism of the Holy Ghost.*

Meyers, F. B., *A Castaway*
Back to Bethel

BIBLIOGRAPHY

Miller, Elmer C., *Pentecost Examined*, Springfield, Missouri, Gospel Publishing House, 1936.

Murray, Andrew, *Full Blessing of Pentecost*.
The Spirit of Christ, London, Nisbet & Co., 1888.

Owen, John, *Discourse Concerning the Spirit*.

Pierson, Dr. A. T., *Acts of the Holy Spirit*.

Simpson, A. B., *The Holy Spirit or Power From on High*, New York, Christian Alliance Publishing Co., 1924.

Tophel, G., *The Work of the Holy Spirit in Man*, Edinburgh, T & T. Clark, 1882.

Torrey, R. A., *Baptism With the Holy Spirit*.
Person and Work of the Holy Spirit.
The Holy Spirit, Who He Is and What He Does.

PASSAGES IN THE BIBLE IN WHICH THERE ARE REFERENCES TO THE HOLY SPIRIT:

Gen. 1:2	2 Sam. 23:1, 2	Isa. 44:3
Gen. 6:3		Isa. 48:16
Gen. 41:38	2 Kings 2:16	Isa. 49:19
		Isa. 49:21
Ex. 28:3	1 Chron. 12:18	Isa. 61:1
Ex. 31:3		Isa. 63:10
Ex. 35:31		Isa. 63:11
	2 Chron. 15:1	Isa. 63:14
	2 Chron. 18:23	
Num. 11:17	2 Chron. 20:14	Ezek. 2:2
Num. 11:25	2 Chron. 24:20	Ezek. 3:12
Num. 11:26		Ezek. 8:3
Num. 11:29	Neh. 9:20	Ezek. 11:1
Num. 24:2	Neh. 9:30	Ezek. 11:5
Num. 27:18		Ezek. 11:19
		Ezek. 11:24
Deut. 34:9	Job 26:13	Ezek. 36:26
	Job 33:4	Ezek. 36:27
		Ezek. 37:1
Judges 3:10	Ps. 51:11	Ezek. 37:14
Judges 6:34	Ps. 51:12	Ezek. 39:29
Judges 11:29	Ps. 104:30	
Judges 13:25	Ps. 139:7	Joel 2:28
Judges 14:6	Ps. 143:10	Joel 2:29
Judges 14:19		
Judges 15:14	Prov. 1:23	Micah 2:7
		Micah 3:8
1 Sam. 10:6		
1 Sam. 10:10	Isa. 11:2	Hag. 2:5
1 Sam. 11:6	Isa. 30:1	
1 Sam. 16:13	Isa. 32:15	
1 Sam. 16:14	Isa. 34:16	Zech. 4:6
1 Sam. 19:20	Isa. 40:7	Zech. 7:12
1 Sam. 19:23	Isa. 42:1	

[194]

References to the Holy Spirit

Zech. 12:10

Mal. 2:15

Matt. 1:18
Matt. 3:11
Matt. 4:1
Matt. 10:20
Matt. 12:18
Matt. 12:28
Matt. 12:31
Matt. 12:32
Matt. 22:43
Matt. 28:20

Mark 1:8
Mark 1:10
Mark 1:12
Mark 3:29
Mark 12:36
Mark 13:11

Luke 1:15
Luke 1:35
Luke 1:41
Luke 1:67
Luke 2:25
Luke 2:26
Luke 2:27
Luke 3:16
Luke 3:22
Luke 4:1
Luke 4:14
Luke 4:18
Luke 10:21
Luke 11:13

Luke 12:10
Luke 12:12
Luke 24:49

John 1:32
John 1:33
John 3:5
John 3:6
John 3:8
John 3:34
John 6:63
John 7:39
John 14:16
John 14:17
John 14:26
John 15:26
John 16:7
John 16:8
John 16:9
John 16:10
John 16:11
John 16:13
John 16:14
John 16:15
John 20:22

Acts 1:2
Acts 1:4
Acts 1:5
Acts 1:8
Acts 1:16
Acts 2:4
Acts 2:17
Acts 2:18
Acts 2:33
Acts 2:38

Acts 4:8
Acts 4:25
Acts 4:31
Acts 5:3
Acts 5:9
Acts 5:32
Acts 6:3
Acts 6:5
Acts 6:10
Acts 7:51
Acts 7:55
Acts 8:15
Acts 8:17
Acts 8:18
Acts 8:19
Acts 8:20
Acts 8:29
Acts 8:39
Acts 9:17
Acts 9:31
Acts 10:19
Acts 10:20
Acts 10:38
Acts 10:44
Acts 10:45
Acts 10:47
Acts 11:12
Acts 11:15
Acts 11:16
Acts 11:24
Acts 13:2
Acts 13:4
Acts 13:9
Acts 13:52
Acts 15:8
Acts 15:28
Acts 16:6

Acts 16:7
Acts 19:2
Acts 19:6
Acts 20:22
Acts 20:23
Acts 20:28
Acts 21:4
Acts 21:11
Acts 28:25

Rom. 1:4
Rom. 5:5
Rom. 8:1
Rom. 8:2
Rom. 8:4
Rom. 8:5
Rom. 8:9
Rom. 8:10
Rom. 8:11
Rom. 8:13
Rom. 8:14
Rom. 8:15
Rom. 8:16
Rom. 8:23
Rom. 8:26
Rom. 8:27
Rom. 14:17
Rom. 15:13
Rom. 15:16
Rom. 15:19
Rom. 15:30

1 Cor. 2:4
1 Cor. 2:10
1 Cor. 2:11
1 Cor. 2:12

1 Cor. 2:13
I Cor. 2:14
1 Cor. 3:16
1 Cor. 6:11
1 Cor. 6:19
1 Cor. 7:40
1 Cor. 12:3
1 Cor. 12:4
1 Cor. 12:7
1 Cor. 12:8
1 Cor. 12:9
1 Cor. 12:11
1 Cor. 12:13
1 Cor. 14:2

2 Cor. 1:22
2 Cor. 3:3
2 Cor. 3:6
2 Cor. 3:8
2 Cor. 3:17
2 Cor. 3:18
2 Cor. 4:13
2 Cor. 5:5
2 Cor. 6:6
2 Cor. 11:4
2 Cor. 12:18
2 Cor. 13:14

Gal. 3:2
Gal. 3:3
Gal. 3:5
Gal. 3:14
Gal. 4:6
Gal. 4:29
Gal. 5:5
Gal. 5:16

Gal. 5:17
Gal. 5:18
Gal. 5:22
Gal. 5:25
Gal. 6:8

Eph. 1:13
Eph. 1:17
Eph. 2:18
Eph. 2:22
Eph. 3:5
Eph. 3:16
Eph. 4:3
Eph. 4:4
Eph. 4:30
Eph. 5:9
Eph. 5:18
Eph. 6:17
Eph. 6:18

Phil. 1:19
Phil. 2:1
Phil. 3:3

Col. 1:8

1 Thess. 1:5
1 Thess. 1:6
1 Thess. 4:8
1 Thess. 5:19

2 Thess. 2:13

1 Tim. 3:16
1 Tim. 4:1

REFERENCES TO THE HOLY SPIRIT

2 Tim. 1:7	1 Peter 1:12	Rev. 1:4
2 Tim. 1:14	1 Peter 1:22	Rev. 1:10
	1 Peter 3:18	Rev. 2:7
Titus 3:5	1 Peter 4:6	Rev. 2:11
	1 Peter 4:14	Rev. 2:17
Heb. 2:4		Rev. 2:29
Heb. 3:7	2 Peter 1:21	Rev. 3:1
Heb. 4:3		Rev. 3:6
Heb. 4:4		Rev. 3:13
Heb. 4:7	1 John 2:20	Rev. 3:22
Heb. 6:4	1 John 2:27	Rev. 4:5
Heb. 9:8	1 John 3:24	Rev 4:5
Heb. 9:14	1 John 4:2	Rev. 5:6
Heb. 10:15	1 John 4:6	Rev. 11:11
Heb. 10:29	1 John 4:13	Rev. 14:11
	1 John 5:7	Rev. 17:3
James 4:5, R. V.	1 John 5:8	Rev. 21:10
		Rev. 22:17
1 Peter 1:2	Jude 19	
1 Peter 1:11	Jude 20	

INDEX OF SUBJECTS

INDEX OF SUBJECTS

[199]

INDEX OF SUBJECTS

INDEX OF TEXTS

INDEX OF TEXTS